Praise for *Immersed*

It truly blesses me to see one of our Harvest School alumni pursuing His God, His Papa. In his book, *Immersed in His Glory*, Michael Lombardo points the way to an intimate relationship with the triune God.

When Jesus had to leave this earth, He sent His best friend, Holy Spirit, to comfort us, to teach us, and to remain so close to us. The key is and always has been intimacy with our Lord through Holy Spirit. In his personal journey as a missionary and lover of God, Michael lives this kind of radical lifestyle; depending solely on what he hears Papa asking.

So you see, church, we're all born to experience His glory. Jesus is patiently waiting to give us more and more. To immerse us deeper and deeper in His glory. Let's continue to pursue this abundance in Him. Read Michael's book, learn and most importantly, enjoy.

Heidi G. Baker, PhD
Co-Founder and CEO of Iris Global

Immersed in His Glory is more than just a book; it is a catalyst into new depths of intimacy with God. Michael Lombardo has done an excellent job revealing beautiful truths of God's grace and goodness that will result in a fresh understanding of just what is possible for those who believe. The book is filled with fresh revelation and insight, and I highly recommend that you read it and know that you were born for more!

Brian Britton
Missionary revivalist and senior pastor of The Dwelling Place
IRIS Virginia

I'm excited to endorse Michael Lombardo's book, *Immersed in His Glory*. Michael gives us insight concerning intimacy with Jesus, and we know that nothing in our lives is worth living or doing without being close to Him. All of us have run after success and fulfillment in the wrong places only to return to our first Love and wonder why we ever strayed away from Him! We have the honor and privilege of being in His presence 24/7, and this book inspires and encourages us to actually live that way. Michael Lombardo is truly a lover of God and a rising voice in this generation.

Roberts Liardon
Pastor, Embassy International Church
Author of over 75 books and the platinum-selling series
God's Generals

Helping you move beyond the mental and emotional hindrances to knowing and receiving from God's presence, *Immersed in His Glory* will serve as a practical and powerful resource in drawing you closer to the Lord. Simplicity is the mark of all true spirituality. That's why I'm glad to know that this work by Michael Lombardo is available. I believe that the Holy Spirit will use this book to stir your faith, intensify your spiritual hunger, renew your mind, and set your soul ablaze with a passionate love for Jesus.

David Diga Hernandez
Evangelist, TV host, and author of *Carriers of the Glory*
www.DavidHernandezMinistries.com

Immersed in His Glory is more than just a book of personal testimonies by the author; it captivates your attention to encounter the Father personally, intimately, and spiritually. Michael Lombardo has outlined a divine template in this book that challenges believers to break through mediocrity, normalcy, and being mundane. Go beyond the natural and become supernatural in your walk with the Lord. *Immersed in His Glory* will change your spiritual palette and appetite for more of Jesus.

Reading *Immersed in His Glory* caused me to reevaluate my own Christian walk, and this well-written, thought-provoking literature will revolutionize your own relationship with the Father. Michael carries an "in season and out of season" prophetic word for this generation that will catapult many to desire more of Jesus. Jesus said that His meat or nourishment was to do the work of the Father who sent Him and finish His work. *Immersed in His Glory* will start you on that spiritual pathway to the finishing line of personal fulfillment, purpose, and destiny.

I highly recommend this book for all readers who may feel stuck in a rut or feel less of themselves, but after reading this amazing book you will know once and for all with assurance that you are *Immersed in His Glory!*

Hakeem Collins
Author of *Heaven Declares* and *Prophetic Breakthrough*

Intimacy and friendship—they go hand in hand. These two virtues were awakened in my spirit as I read *Immersed in His Glory* by Michael Lombardo. It is a beautifully written testimony of life coupled with passionate searching of the Word of God. If you want to dive into the knowledge of God's immense love, presence, and His desire to enter into a divine romance in eternal communion with *you, this* is the book for you.

Jason Lee Jones
Senior leader of the Godbreed Company
IRIS Savannah

I love and respect Michael Lombardo. I know him to be a passionate disciple of Jesus Christ, following Him wherever He leads. I love his love for people all over the world. I truly believe he is leaving a legacy in the hearts of all who meet and experience him.

Lyle Phillips
Lead Pastor, Legacy Nashville
Founder of Mercy29

When I think of Michael, I think of these words—a radical lover of Jesus, an individual who has an immense hunger for God's Word, and also extraordinary gift of compassion for hurting people. He is a prolific writer with a supernatural gift of communication, and he is serious about the call of God on his life. I have no hesitation in saying that he and Selina are called to the kingdom for such a time as this and will both be used by God to reach thousands.

Sharon Hobbs
Professor, Outreaches and House of Prayer Director
Christ for the Nations Institute

Michael is writing from his heart with a desire to bring you into more depth and understanding of a living God, our Creator and Lover, our King and Friend. By writing from his personal journey, he is drawing you in to ask questions relevant to a fresh perspective of the kingdom and your place in it.

Byron Easterling
Bonaire Initiative/Bontir.com Bhh, Inc.

Michael Lombardo has always carried a fresh hunger and word that is contagious. This book will produce the same in you!

Chris Estrada
Director of Youth Ministries
Christ for the Nations Institute
Author of *Finisher*
www.chrisestrada.tv

Immersed in His Glory is a testimony of how God can radically change a self-centered life to a life completely dedicated to the Lordship of Jesus Christ. More than just a personal testimony, it is a book that clearly is written from out of personal journey and intimate encounters with Jesus. Michael unveils the truth that when someone truly seeks a close walk with God they will find it. It is a challenge to go beyond the nominal, laid-back Christian lifestyle to a deeper encounter with the Father. I am so impressed with Michael's depth and clarity of revelation. It clearly displays his own personal experiences in his walk with God. It also serves as the platform for his appeal to the body of Christ to seek a deeper and more meaningful encounter with God. Michael so pointedly writes that we need "an encounter with Jesus that revolutionizes everything." You are going to not only be blessed, but you will be challenged as you find out that you were *born for more.*

Dr. David T. Demola
Pastor, Faith Fellowship Ministries World Outreach Center
Sayreville, New Jersey
President, Covenant Ministries International

In his book, Immersed in His Glory, Michael Lombardo reveals the glorious truth that we can live in and carry the manifest glory of God on our lives. Sharing from his personal journey and scripture Michael teaches how to access a lifestyle of God's presence through the grace and rest of God. You will be free from self-striving and empowered to enter into a greater depth of intimacy with God. This is a great book that will renew your mind with truth on what God's grace really does for you! I love it!

Matt Sorger
International Speaker & Author
Founder of Rescue1
Mattsorger.com

IMMERSED

IN HIS

Glory

DESTINY IMAGE® PUBLISHERS, INC.
P.O. Box 310, Shippensburg, PA 17257-0310
"Promoting Inspired Lives."

Previously published as *Born for More* by Life Poured Out Publications
Previous ISBN: 978-0-9974202-0-3

This book and all other Destiny Image and Destiny Image Fiction books are available at Christian bookstores and distributors worldwide.

Cover design by: Eileen Rockwell

For more information on foreign distributors, call 717-532-3040.
Reach us on the Internet: www.destinyimage.com.

ISBN 13 TP: 978-0-7684-1778-4
ISBN 13 eBook: 978-0-7684-1779-1
ISBN 13 HC: 978-0-7684-1780-7
ISBN 13 LP: 978-0-7684-1781-4

For Worldwide Distribution, Printed in the U.S.A.
1 2 3 4 5 6 7 8 / 22 21 20 19 18

This book is dedicated to my beloved wife,

Selina Michelle Lombardo.

I'm eternally grateful that God lovingly chose you to be my wife.

You are truly brilliant, tenderhearted, godly, anointed, multi-gifted, and the greatest encourager in my life.

You are my partner, my equal, and my radiant bride.

You have helped me through the entire process of getting this message to the world and you have always believed in me.

Thank you.

I love you Selina with all of my heart.

Acknowledgments

To my father and mother, Joseph and Stephanie Lombardo. You've stood by my side and believed in me against all odds. You've loved me unconditionally, prayed for me unceasingly, and taught me God's Word from my childhood. The fruit in my life is a product of all you've sown into me. I love you both with all my heart!

To my sisters Danielle and Michelle, and my brother Joe: you've encouraged and supported me time and time again with the call of God on my life. Thank you.

To my brother-in-law Rene: God used you to give me a glimpse of what He's really like before I ever knew Him. I'm happy to call you my brother, and I'm proud of all you are doing for the kingdom of God.

To my aunt Angela: you're one of the most reliable people that I know. You've always been quick to help me with whatever I've needed, and you've done it with gladness and sincerity. Thank you for everything.

To my pastors David and Diane Demola: you've invested so much into my family. Pastor Dave, you're a bold example of a man of God who lives by faith, and you are a father to the nations. Thank you for everything, we're proud to call you our pastors.

To Sharon Hobbs: you saw the call on my life and you encouraged, nurtured, corrected, and instructed me like a true spiritual mother. You took me on my first mission trip, and I was forever changed. You are amazing and an inspiration to many.

Acknowledgments

To Brian and Candice Simmons: throughout the entire process of writing and publishing you've been there to answer my questions, offer advice, and point me in the right direction to see this God-given dream come to fruition. It's an honor to serve you and glean from the revelation and experience of you both. You are a power team for the kingdom of God, and an extraordinary example for this generation.

To our supporters around the world: thank you to everyone who has partnered with us through prayer and faithful giving into our mission efforts. Because of your Christ-like generosity, lives have been touched and transformed around the world. You're always in our hearts and prayers.

Most importantly, I want to thank Father, Son, and Holy Spirit. I love You, because You first loved me. Without You, life would be meaningless. You are my joy and the delight of my life. Serving You is my honor and greatest pleasure.

You have my life now and forever.

Contents

Foreword

You were born for more than status quo Christianity! God's calling on your life runs deep—like a river. He has invested sacred blood to purchase your soul. He has placed His Holy Spirit within you like a fountain and a spring. He has blessed you beyond measure. Yes, you were born for more!

It's time for the church to awaken to our high calling and be the light of the world, shining into every corner of darkness. Our destiny is greater than simply having a successful business or ministry—it is to be a co-ruler with Jesus Christ at His right hand. Can you see your life as preparation for this calling? All that you have passed through has prepared you for such a time as this. Every time I find my heart turning away from this glorious destiny, all I have to do is to remember what God has done for me. The past points us to our eternal destiny of finding the "more" of God.

Michael Lombardo has written an amazing new book that is destined to be an incredible tool for many a Christian. It includes a lot of his own personal stories of failures and successes. After his powerful conversion experience, an inner war was waged as he began wearing the trappings of religion and self-sufficiency as his new armor. This ultimately kept the fullness of the Holy Spirit from flowing freely in his life. At that point, he was miserable as he lived in the dead, dry doctrine of the Law. Nothing he did—acts of service, tireless hours of prayer—

nothing was able to satisfy the longing in his heart for more. Little did he realize that religion had become a wall keeping him back from what his heart was truly longing for the most. Religion held his feelings and emotions at bay, allowing him to be fed the lies of the enemy. Has that ever happened to you? Then God began to call him out into deeper waters, and so the quest began.

His heart began to yearn for so much more of God, but he lacked the wherewithal on how to pursue communion with Him and abide in this amazing reality. Over time, as the glory of God's presence came pouring in like a flood, he began to realize how much he was missing out on all along. This is the soul intent of this book. Michael will take you through the steps for reaching into the treasure house of God. As he moves forward in his quest he takes you along with him. It's time to discover God's dream for your life! And it's time to live each day in the glory! The Father desires to share His secrets with you. It's time for you to establish a close, personal relationship with the triune God. The Father wants to let you in on the secrets of the universe.

With a keen understanding of spiritual truths, Michael gives you insights which will aid you on your journey. If you're one that longs for a deep and rich personal relationship, I can guarantee that you will develop one as you begin to understand and practice the steps found in this life-changing book. Religion and spiritual pride have blinded many a well-meaning believer. The enemy has used the same lie century after century and has stolen, killed, and destroyed (John 10:10) many a destiny while holding believers captive till they are found languishing in his religious cages. Today is your day to be completely set free and to experience the depths of His heart! Come and experience Him in the pages of this book. Your friend, your lover, and bridegroom King has set His affection on you, so come. Let's discover who He truly is. He wants to be the lover of your soul and the fiery seal upon your heart! Let the wonderful adventure begin!

Brian Simmons
Stairway Ministries
The Passion Translation Project
www.stairwayministries.org
www.thepassiontranslation.com

Introduction
My Story

Growing up, I would tell my mother that I hated reading. In turn, she would remind me of the time when I was roughly eight years old and read the word *inconsequential* by myself. That story really irked me, but she never failed to mention it when I didn't want to open up my summer reading books for school.

When I got saved, new desires started to develop in me. I suddenly wanted to read my Bible for hours every day. I also wanted to read books from various ministers who would build my faith, and out of nowhere I had this strange desire to write books. It was extremely difficult to wrap my mind around, but I couldn't shake the thought. Instead of shrugging it off, I decided to seriously seek the Lord about it until I got my answer.

You may ask, "What did you do?" Well, I determined to do something drastic. First I waited for the sun to go down. The reason for this was to conquer my fear of being alone in the dark, forcing myself to trust God. Next, I took about a thirty-minute walk through my neighborhood, into the woods, and up a steep hill to seek God there until He cleared away the obscurities about this matter. Off I went into the dark with unswerving faith to seek Him regarding my destiny. Finally, I made it to the top with my flashlight in one hand and my Bible in the other. *Now what?* I thought to myself. After a bit, I decided to open my Bible, read a random Psalm, and ask God about the feelings I was having. Fifteen minutes passed and I was bored stiff, and honestly a bit scared. More time passed and I decided to head back to my house. I stood up, reached the peak of the hill, and began my descent when suddenly I heard the small, yet authoritative, voice of God say, *Seven years.* Those words rang loud and clear through my spirit. I took hold of them and rejoiced all the way home. In preparation, I determined to write down every revelation I would receive from Scripture, and journal the encounters I had in the Spirit from that day forward.

With this commitment also came opposition. The devil wasn't pleased with the new fruit that was springing up from my newfound relationship with Christ. In high school, ecstasy was one of my favorite drugs. It wasn't until later that I realized how damaging the effects would be on my brain. In time, I actually developed a minor stutter. On top of that, I noticed my thoughts were more cluttered and less coherent than they used to be. When I sat down to write, I would struggle with the words to express myself, which had never been an issue before. The devil would then seize the opportunity and whisper all kinds of lies into my head like, *You'll never write. You'll never be a mouthpiece for God. Just give up. You're stupid. God can't use you.* Depression came rushing in like a flood and hopelessness rested on my shoulders like a heavy garment. Then suddenly, within the darkness, a light arose within me. A voice spoke that had the power to shatter a thousand lies. God told me to open my Bible to see what He had to say about the matter. I'll never forget the Scripture that He led me to. It's been one I've stood on and still stand on in writing this book.

"My heart is stirred by a noble theme as I recite my verses for the king; **my tongue is the pen of a skillful writer"**

(Psalm 45:1 NIV).

During one of my private devotions with the Lord while I was going through this time, His presence manifested sweetly, yet powerfully. I was sitting on my couch, and the next thing I knew, currents of His presence pulsated through my brain. By the Spirit within me, I knew it was Father God restoring health to my brain from years of drug abuse. Then my heart opened to receive, and I told Him, "I receive, Daddy. I receive your healing touch." From that moment on, it's happened more times than I can recount. To this day, I can confidently and unreservedly tell you that my stutter is gone and my ability to think, speak, write, and innovate is greater than ever before. Not only did Father God restore me entirely, He gave me double for everything the devil had stolen!

The revelations I'm going to share in this book are things that the Lord has taught me over the years. I'm excited to step into another level of God's faithfulness in this writing endeavor. As I felt Holy Spirit release me to write this book, Scripture was becoming more alive to me than ever before on these topics. I felt like an awe-struck student at the feet of the most brilliant teacher, and indeed I have been. "A pupil is not above his teacher; but everyone, after he has been fully trained, will be like his teacher" (Luke 6:40). My life's ambition is to remain a student of our glorious Teacher and King, so that I can be conformed into all that He is! These truths have reshaped and reformed me. In this season, I've allowed them to challenge my heart afresh and penetrate the deepest parts of who I am. My goal for those reading this book is that these truths will take root in your heart through faith and that Jesus will be glorified through you, His glorious bride.

Chapter 1

Destined for Glory

"It was for this He called you through our gospel, that you may gain the glory of our Lord Jesus Christ"

(2 Thessalonians 2:14).

Every human being is destined for the glory of God. It's impossible to step into the fullness of your destiny unless the Holy Spirit comes and saturates you with His holy presence. What makes Christianity stand alone from all the other religions of the world is that we have a tangible God who longs to reveal Himself to us. Our Father yearns to pour out His Spirit on those who are hungry for Him. When you come to the place in your walk with God where you begin to think, "There has to be more than this…" you are the perfect candidate for a deeper encounter with Jesus Christ. Even if you've experienced Him in amazing ways—*there is always more*. Do you want to experience more of God?

While many are trying to claw their way into the presence of God through various spiritual practices, Jesus has carried us into heaven's fullness by no merit of our own. Through this book, I aim to bring forth revelations that have changed my life entirely. As you allow them to penetrate your heart also, I strongly believe they will do the same for you. My goal is to share truth that will liberate you from common hindrances in your pursuit of more of God. Together we will explore revelation that will empower you to walk through the mysterious yet glorious terrain of divine union with Jesus. By the end of this book, you will be fully prepared to experience God's presence in greater measures and to abide in His glory twenty-four seven.

To many, this may sound blasphemous, but you were *created for glory*. As a woman is man's glory (1 Corinthians 11:7), Jesus' bride (the church) is His glory. Mankind was created to be glory-carriers and image-bearers of our Triune God. Through Christ, you've become a recipient of His divine life, you've been brought into oneness with Jesus (1 Corinthians 6:17), and have received the same glory that Jesus has with the Father (John 17:22). If you think that's great, just wait, we have a lot more ground to excavate.

Grace, Love, and Presence

The apostle Paul ended his second epistle to the Corinthian church with the blessing of all blessings. "The grace of the Lord Jesus Christ, and the love of God, and the fellowship of the Holy Spirit, be with you all" (2 Corinthians 13:14). In this benediction, Paul unveiled God's undying passion in exposing aspects of Himself to us that are vital to our spiritual strength and well-being. Obtaining these three living revelations of grace, love, and presence is the power behind fulfilling our God-ordained destinies. The Amplified Bible says it like this, "*The grace* (favor and spiritual blessing) *of the Lord Jesus Christ* and *the love of God* and *the presence and fellowship* (the communion and sharing together, and participation) *in the Holy Spirit* be with you all. *Amen (so be it)*" (2 Corinthians 13:14 AMP).

In my own journey with the Lord, which I'll share in greater detail throughout this book, the Lord has opened my spiritual eyes to the all-encompassing power of these three essential revelations. I want to explore and unpack these realties, because I believe it's impossible to experience more of God's glory without awakening to His outrageous love, His unfathomable grace, and cultivating an intimate relationship with Holy Spirit.

Some believers understand God's love for them, but they lack the imperative revelation of His empowering grace. God loves us unconditionally, even in our sinfulness—but He loves us so much He refuses to keep us there. Grace is the presence of Jesus in our lives that enables us to live just like Him in the earth.

Other believers may have a theological understanding of God's love and grace, yet they leave the Holy Spirit out of the equation. The Holy Spirit can be the most ignored person in the church today. Some people would rather play church, sing a couple songs, give their tithe, hear a neatly packaged sermon, and move on with their lives. But where's the Holy Spirit in our midst?

Jesus told His disciples to do nothing and stay put until they received the promise of the Father—*the Person of the Spirit*. The Holy Spirit isn't an "it." He isn't an ethereal force. He's a person. He's the substance and tangibility of God. We grow to understand Christ by the agency of the Spirit alone. You've never encountered Jesus, received revelation of Scripture, or moved in the gifts of God without Holy Spirit's operation.

With all of this talk about the "presence" of God in certain church circles, many may wonder where this can be found in the Bible. For example, "In Your presence is fullness of joy; in Your right hand there are pleasures forever" (Psalm 16:11). You can also use the words *Spirit* and *presence* interchangeably throughout Scripture. For example, "Walk by the Spirit, and you will not carry out the desire of the flesh." (Galatians 5:16) As a believer you are always in the Spirit, but you're not always walking in the Spirit. Learning to abide in the presence of God is learning to walk in the Spirit. The Spirit of God wraps around you in a manifest way to make the invisible realm tangible within the visible realm. He takes what is unseen and causes it to materialize in our earthly experience. In other words, you can actually *feel* God. In fact, He is passionate about you encountering His presence in an experiential way.

Roadblocks to "More"

There are many beliefs that have instilled paralyzing fear in God's people, which have victimized the church from the beginning. Some believe that the baptism of the Spirit and the gifts of the Spirit have passed away with the first apostles and aren't active today.

I met a young man a few years back that loved debating doctrine. Every time I saw him in a social setting he was inciting conversation about predestination, once saved always saved, or discounting the reality of hell. He also held firm to the belief system called cessationism (that the gifts of the Spirit are no longer active today). I was very familiar with these doctrines, so I often spoke with him, trying to show him the pure love and truth of Jesus. One night I felt strongly impressed by the Spirit to cease my discussions with him and to ask one simple question, "Have you ever been hurt by charismatics or disappointed with God in any way?" Immediately, his whole demeanor changed. He opened up to me about feeling pressured to speak in tongues and engage in certain spiritual activities. These negative encounters drove him to his knees, praying, "Lord, if this is real, give me a sign." He didn't sense an immediate response, so he shunned the Spirit altogether and clung to the lie of cessationism to justify his lack of experience in God. Any bit of faith he had was squashed by doubt and disappointment.

Others believe in the Holy Spirit and His activity today, but they draw back from fully giving themselves to Him for various reasons. Some fear man's opinion, while others simply fear what they don't understand. Instead of remaining open to whatever the Spirit of God would like to do, they choose to live safely without the possibility of suffering the ridicule of others or being uncomfortable. Understand this: the mark of true spiritual maturity isn't "weirdness." Yet, it's imperative to know that God cares less about you saving face and more about your freedom in Him!

I was teaching a class on the Holy Spirit to an international Bible school in New Jersey. Towards the end of class, I made sure to put on some worship and allow the students to engage with the Spirit about the issues of their heart. While they were praying and communing with Him, I noticed a young girl crying in my peripheral vision. At the end of the class she testified of how God ministered to her during that time. She told the class that she was always scared of the Holy Spirit. She didn't know that He was kind, loving, and desired spiritual intimacy with her. She imagined Him to be weird, impersonal, and controlling.

Through the teaching and prayer, she was set free to trust in the Holy Spirit's love and goodness. She finally let go of her preconceived notions of Him and fully yielded herself into His everlasting arms. Jesus is beautiful!

There are also many believers in the world who aren't Spirit-filled. Yes, they received the Holy Spirit when they first believed, but they've yet to receive the baptism of the Spirit. In John 20, Jesus appeared to His disciples for the first time after He resurrected from the dead. Faith sprung up in their hearts as they beheld Him in His glorified form and Jesus responded by breathing on them saying, *"Receive the Holy Spirit."* Later in Acts 1, Jesus told the disciples to wait until they were baptized in the Spirit in order for them to become true witnesses of the gospel in love and power. Looking into these Scriptures we can see that they first received the Holy Spirit in John 20 when they first believed, but later they were baptized in the Spirit in Acts 2 on the day of Pentecost.

In Acts 19, the apostle Paul asked a group of believers if they received the Spirit when they got saved. It turned out that they knew nothing of the Holy Spirit—and Paul, in turn, laid hands on them to receive Him. I know many people who are true believers in Christ, but they haven't been filled with the Spirit yet. They have attended church services where the Spirit of God was flowing and because this was foreign to them, they hardened their hearts towards Him altogether. It's critical that our hearts remain soft and open to whatever God desires to do in us and through us—regardless of what it looks like to the natural eye. Never let what you don't understand hold you back from experiencing the fullness of your spiritual inheritance in Christ. Tell God, *"If it's you, I want it! I don't care what it looks like!"* It is amazing how quickly God begins to move in your life when you ask Him to have His way in you!

To others, the very thought of surrendering full control to God and letting the Spirit take the wheel is terrifying, to say the least. They feel they must maintain control of their lives and in doing so they restrict God's hand from operating as He pleases. The root of seeking control is distrust in God's nature. When we choose to distrust God, fear is the unhealthy byproduct. As fear puts its roots down into our hearts, the natural response is to seize control of our lives, the lives of others, and our circumstances. Learning to trust in God's nature and kind-intentions will set you free from the fear that dominates you. Knowing His love towards you—that He's always working for your good and constantly has your best in mind—will free you to give the Spirit total control in all things!

The Barrier of Head Knowledge

"Knowledge makes arrogant, but love edifies" (1 Corinthians 8:1). Building up your mind is entirely different from feeding your spirit. Many scholars and theologians pride themselves in their tidy doctrines but lack the heart behind the doctrine. Heidi Baker, a hero of mine, often says, "Our head is too big, and our heart is too small."

In her monumental book, *Compelled by Love*, she shares a story of when she ministered at Harvard University among some of the most brilliant minds alive right now. A young man was touched by her message on feeling like an orphan to Father God, and he came to the front for prayer.

He desperately wanted to know God, but he said his mind was too strong. So, Heidi prayed that his heart would expand even larger than his incredible mind. During this prayer, she called one of the church leaders over to hug him because she felt Daddy God wanted to embrace him. Later on in the service she witnessed firsthand this young man worshiping God with all of his heart and might! He was saying, "I feel God! I feel God! He is so strong!"[1]

During my time at Christ for the Nations Institute in Dallas Texas, I met many precious lovers of God. CFNI is chock full of young people who hunger after God and wholeheartedly dream to make a lasting impact in this world with the gospel of Jesus Christ. However, where there are genuine believers, there are also bad apples hidden within the love feast. There was a group of guys who spent a majority of their time debating with other students about heavy subjects of doctrine. These guys didn't carry love as the atmosphere of their lives, but walked around haughtily with their noses to the sky. Pride is a killer—it puffs up. But receiving the love of God will fashion humility and integrity within you, which is essential to your life in Christ.

Now, there is nothing wrong with conversations about doctrine and spiritual realities for sharpening one another in the faith. But these guys were always debating, arguing, and causing more people to stumble then embrace the truth of God. One guy in particular always sparked conversation with me in hopes that I'd engage in discussion with him. I felt that it was important not to get distracted in that way but to show him the love of God. I'd simply smile at him and tell him, "It's all about Jesus my brother. Let's walk in

Him, love Him, draw near to Him, and live Him in the world. That's what I want more than anything else." He'd throw a few rebuttals my way like, "Yes, that's true, but we need to watch over our doctrine," or, "we must rightly divide the Word." When he saw that I wasn't budging, he'd back off and move onto his next victim. The next thing I knew, he started to approach me with a different attitude. Suddenly, he wasn't starting a theological debate, but he was truly seeking insight into the heart of God.

One afternoon he invited me over to his apartment to talk, so I gladly accepted the invitation. I'll never forget what transpired that afternoon. He looked me square in the eyes, and with his enormous study Bible in hand he said, "Michael, I read this book to gain knowledge, sort out my doctrinal stances and build arguments so I can convince people that they are wrong in their beliefs and that I am right. After talking with you a few times I noticed something very different about you. Through you I witness genuine love. You carry God's presence, and that's what I'm missing. I have come to learn that it's what I truly want and need more than anything!" Right then, I put my hands on his shoulders and blessed him for his vulnerability and repentant attitude. From that day onward, I saw a remarkable, Spirit- filled change take place in his life. He grew leaps and bounds in the realm of the Spirit. He was oozing with the love of God and stopped the trivial debating. He embraced real faith in Christ! Not the head kind of faith, but the heart kind. Human faith can only take you so far. You need the God kind of faith that seizes your heart and compels you into the deeper things of the kingdom.

The Glory of the Lord

From Genesis to Revelation, God's heart to dwell physically among His people is evidently seen. Genesis begins with God creating man and woman to dwell with Him in unhindered, intimate fellowship. Once that relationship was severed, you see God revealing Himself to those whose hearts were hungry for Him. From Abraham being justified by faith, Moses experiencing the reality of intimate friendship with God, and David living in the holy emotions of the Almighty, God's heart shines from each page. His overarching passion to break into the natural realm and captivate the hearts of His people is manifest all throughout the Scriptures.

The Bible teaches about the twofold presence of God. You have the omnipresence and manifest presence of God. God is omnipresent, meaning that He is everywhere at all times. There isn't one place that He isn't. Literally, He takes up all the space. He's in the church down the street, the bar around the corner, your cubicle at work, and in distant galaxies all at the same time. He's with you everywhere you go, whether you feel Him or not. It doesn't matter if you are aware of His movements around you, He's there and actively involved.

"Where could I go from your Spirit? Where could I run and hide from your face? If I go up to heaven, you're there! If I go down to the realm of the dead, you're there too! If I fly with wings into the shining dawn, you're there! If I fly into the radiant sunset, you're there waiting! Wherever I go, your hand will

*guide me; your strength will empower me. It's
impossible to disappear from you or to ask the
darkness to hide me; for your presence is everywhere
bringing light into my night!"*

(Psalm 139:7-11 TPT)

It doesn't matter if you're running from the Lord; there
is nowhere you can hide. If you're planning to escape to the
bar downtown to drown away your sorrows, *there He is
calling you home.* Maybe you're feeling alone and
downtrodden because you've recently been hurt by
someone close to you—*God's there with you drawing you to
Himself.* He's waiting to lavish His love-gift of grace upon
your fettered heart. Many believe the delusion that God
only dwells in places He is honored. Yes, His manifest
presence fills atmospheres where He is lifted up and
honored. But His presence is everywhere—even among
those who *hate Him.* Mankind can't hide from the glorious
King of kings. He's the chaser and pursuer of the sheep, and
He'll seek us among the muck and mire to lift us up and
seat us with princes in His glory!

The second kind of presence the Bible speaks about is
the *manifest presence of God,* which is often referred to
as *His glory.* The glory of God cannot be contrived or
manufactured. The manifest presence is the Person of the
Holy Spirit bringing heaven's reality to earth. Christ, through
His finished work, has made the manifest presence of God
available to all humanity. We've been ushered effortlessly
back into our life-union with God through what Jesus has
vicariously accomplished for us by putting away our sin.
Jesus has brought the manifest presence of God back to those

who are bold and brave enough to forsake the false identity of the flesh-life and put their trust entirely in Him. Amazingly, God takes what is unseen (omnipresence), and awakens our senses to enter into its reality (manifest presence). God's glory is His revealed, tangible presence among men, experienced within the physical, natural realm.

The tabernacle of Moses dwelt smack dab in the center of Israel, and that's where God's glory dwelt for all to see and experience. An aerial view of the tabernacle reveals that the shape in which it was structured was in the shape of a cross. How magnificent! *It was the cross that brought us back into God's presence.* Every room and article of the tabernacle, including the ark of the covenant itself, was a symbolic picture of our sacrificial Lamb, Jesus Christ. The ark of God's presence unveils the heart of the Father in dwelling among His people to intimately commune with them.

In the Old Testament, you'll often see God's glory manifest and people respond by standing in awe or lying prostrate on their faces in holy fear and reverence. Supreme outbreaks of God's presence are also recorded in the New Testament. For example, when the Spirit of God fell upon the believers on Pentecost, they appeared to be drunk on wine! From Genesis to Revelation the supernatural works of God fill the pages. These amazing encounters weren't merely reserved for the people of that time, but these amazing experiences are still taking place all over the world today! I am grateful that God's presence is substance—it's touchable, it's discernable, and fills our human experience with grace and glory! Are you hungry for His manifest presence?

Gaining His Glory

Did you know you were born again to gain the glory of Christ? Let me prove it.

> *"It was for this He called you through our gospel, that you may **gain the glory** of our Lord Jesus Christ"*
>
> (2 Thessalonians 2:14).

This is a striking statement made by the apostle Paul. Hearing this, many believers get an inner twinge because they've been taught that God won't share His glory with another. How is that possible if the very reason we've been called to God through the gospel is to gain His glory? The Scripture about God not sharing His glory is found in Isaiah 42. The context of this chapter is God choosing Jesus to bring justice and redemption to the world. It's a Messianic prophecy that's been fulfilled through Christ.

> *"Behold, My Servant, whom I uphold; My chosen one in whom My soul delights. I have put My Spirit upon Him; He will bring forth justice to the nations...I am the Lord, I have called You in righteousness, I will also hold You by the hand and watch over You, and I will appoint You as a covenant to the people, as a light to the nations"*
>
> (Isaiah 42:1, 6).

Undeniably, Jesus is the One called in righteousness and appointed as a covenant to the people and a light to the nations. Now, the infamous statement comes, "I am the Lord, that is My name; I will not give My glory to another, nor My praise to graven images." (Isaiah 42:8) There it is! The Lord will never share His glory with Mohammed,

Buddha, Krishna, or the other millions of man-made "gods" fabricated through our vain imaginations and demonic influences. There is only one Way, one Truth, and one Life. Jesus Christ is the true Door into eternal life and no one can see the Father unless they go through Him. God won't share His glory with any other so-called "god," but He will adorn His beloved ones with honor, praise, and glory forever.

The Scriptures are abundantly clear that Jesus died to restore glory back to His inglorious fallen creation. Ichabod, in the Scriptures means, "the glory has departed," and Christ came to reverse the fall's vicious consequences. The glory came when Christ came. You don't need to cry out for His glory to "fall" upon you. That's a pre-Christ, old-covenant prayer. The glory descended in the Person of Jesus Christ and hasn't left because *He lives within you through the Holy Spirit.*

So many believers have a love for God, attend church regularly, and try hard to do what's best in any given situation. They may even serve at church and stand out to many as dedicated followers of Christ. *Yet, there is more.* God is inviting you into the secret chamber of His heart, and asking you for access into the private chamber of yours. Intimacy is what so many are missing. A lifestyle of hearing His words, experiencing His presence, and releasing His kingdom is foreign or may even seem out of reach for many. This book is an invitation into the "more of God" that you're internally aching for. Going through the motions won't give you what your heart truly needs. Church alone can't supply a remedy for your deep-seated dissatisfaction. Only His presence can. *You were created for His presence. Nothing else will do.*

In my travels around the world I've been saddened and burdened to see so many pure hearted, genuine believers struggle in their relationship with the Lord. I'm not only talking about your casual churchgoer. I'm talking about men and women who have left everything behind to follow Jesus and preach the gospel to the lost. They've left family, friends, churches, and high-paying jobs to pour out their lives in third world countries for the poor and destitute. Right before my eyes they've confessed their confusion, vented their frustration, and wept bitterly because of perceived failure in their pursuit of knowing and serving God with all of their heart.

God's heart is hurting over His children who are riddled with unbelief and constrained by their false perceptions of Him. Religion is a brutal and vicious thief that has stolen from Christ's bride far too long. Jesus is broken over His beautiful, lovely bride who is held back by shame, guilt, and self-condemnation. Enough is enough. The Spirit of God is breathing upon the hearts of His people around the world and divinely imparting the revelation of the love of God, the grace of Christ, and the magnificent glory of the Holy Spirit.

"Awake, sleeper, and arise from the dead, and Christ will shine on you"

(Ephesians 5:14).

Let His love overtake you, His grace empower you, and His presence to be your daily enjoyment.

Chapter 2

The Pleasures of God

"In Your presence is fullness of joy; in Your right hand there are pleasures forever"

(Psalm 16:11).

You were created by God, and He wants you to enjoy the beauty of His presence forever. An incredible supernatural journey lies ahead of you as you yield your heart daily to His divine life. Are you ready to move forward on this adventure of a lifetime?

The pleasures of God's presence flow mightily as you learn to lean on Christ with total surrender and absolute trust. Lovingly, your heavenly Father is drawing you into a deeper level of experience in Him. He wants your spirit, soul, and body to be immersed in the beauty of who He is. Why settle for going through the religious motions when God has so much more for you?

The Garden of Pleasure

Let's look back for a moment to the Garden of Eden. It's imperative to see what transpired there because that's where humanity's story began. In the beginning, God created the heavens and the earth. On the earth, He created a garden called Eden. According to the Strong's Lexicon, the name *Eden* in Hebrew is *aden*,[1] literally translated "pleasure" or "delight." God made a garden that was breathtakingly gorgeous, and out of the inspiration of His infinite mind He named it the Garden of Pleasure and Delight. *And it was there that He chose to place humanity.*

What made this garden so full of pleasure? Was it the exotic animals or the abundant plant life and vegetation? What about the trees bearing all kinds of juicy, succulent fruit? I'm sure those things all played their roles, but I believe it was so much more. Adam and Eve walked freely in the presence of God, who is love (1 John 4:8), peace (Philippians 4:7), and goodness (Exodus 33:19). His weighty glory and manifest presence filled every fiber of that garden until every living creature couldn't help but praise Him! (Psalm 150:6) Imagine this, Jesus said even the rocks will cry out if God's people keep quiet!

The Garden of Eden is where God resided with His beloved children without hindrance or separation. Eternal love poured out of the realm of glory into the hearts of Adam and Eve as they gazed with unveiled eyes on the transcendent beauty of the Trinity. His pure light sent waves of peace and joy into their souls. They were completely wrapped in heaven's acceptance and adoration as they walked in union with the Godhead in the cool of the day. God's plan from the beginning wasn't for this reality to be contained in one location. In actuality, He hungered for a day when the whole earth would be filled with this heavenly paradise. The day has dawned and is continuing to unfold as the knowledge of God's glory covers the earth as the waters cover the sea.

Idolatry

All of humanity was born to live in God's glory, just as in the days of Adam and Eve. And until this need is met in

Jesus, we scrounge around ardently searching for anyone or anything to fulfill our God-given needs. But the truth of the matter is that nothing can truly scratch this inner itch, and no one can fill the God-shaped hole within us that craves Him more than life. You were made purposely to need Him. Like it or not, it's the truth. Creation is absolutely dependent upon the Creator. Even the world itself is held together by the word of His power (Hebrews 1:3). Believers and unbelievers alike are both seeking tirelessly for happiness and fulfillment, which cannot be found apart from wholehearted abandonment to Jesus Christ, who is our life.

People are looking for jobs, relationships, money, substances, fame, you name it, to satisfy this deep-seated longing to be restored to their heavenly Father. You may or may not voice your desires out loud but I guarantee you've thought at one point or another, *I won't be happy until I get this big promotion at work*, or *I'm going to be unfulfilled until I meet my spouse*, or maybe, *I need a large ministry and reputation to truly be accomplishing something for the Lord*. Those are all debilitating lies from the devil. The pursuit of happiness apart from relationship with Jesus is called idolatry. Period. I don't like tiptoeing around reality and sugarcoating what the Bible unashamedly declares to be true. The Bible uses this term without repentance. Sadly, some pastors and leaders have become shy about using such terms because they fear man's opinion more than the Lord's Truth. In Old Testament days, God commanded the prophets and righteous kings to lop down the idols that stole away the hearts of His people. In the same way, pastors and leaders need to tear down these same idols. Today, in most cases, they aren't physical altars to false gods. Instead, they are idols we've erected in our hearts that take the place of our preeminent and matchless King Jesus. C.S. Lewis brilliantly stated, "God cannot give us happiness and peace apart from Himself because it is not there. There is no such thing."[2] Only in the presence of the Lord is there fullness of joy and at His right hand eternal pleasures forevermore (Psalm 16:11).

Life is fickle and full of ups and downs. One minute you're on top of the world, the next minute you're in the darkest valley. If your joy and fulfillment is found in "things," then what happens when those things are taken away? You're left empty and broken, seeking for something else as a replacement. Jesus is your only constant in life. He never changes. He's the same yesterday and today and forever (Hebrews 13:8). A person, place, or thing may be taken from you in life, but no one can take Christ away from you. In the book of Genesis, we read that Joseph experienced many ups and downs throughout his lifetime. Through it all, it didn't matter if he was in a pit or in a palace. Do you know why? Because the Bible says that *God was with him*. God's presence was the treasure and reward of Joseph's life. Let's loose our soul attachment to the things of this world, and seek Him alone who is worthy of all praise!

> *"Whom have I in heaven but You! You're all I want! No one on earth means as much to me as You"*
>
> (Psalms 73:25 TPT).

My Journey…

Growing up, I was a partier, drug abuser, womanizer, and rebel. My teenage years were spent chasing carnal pleasure. If it made me high, I wanted to try it—like a true hedonist. A hedonist is someone who seeks pleasure and sensual self-indulgence above all else. The lifestyle I was living was fun for a period of time, but it eventually took a serious toll on me. My parents would tell me that they feel God's presence and even hear Him speak to them. Because I never had such an encounter, I thought they were crazy— *Jesus freaks.*

Because I didn't want to face reality, I shrugged off any sign of God's hand in my life as a coincidence. My perception of God as a teenager was warped and delusional. I imagined Him as more of a cosmic killjoy who wanted to steal all my fun and sit me in a boring church service every Sunday morning. Nothing about living as a Christian was appealing to me whatsoever. My eyes were veiled and I couldn't see Him for who He truly is. All I knew was that God hated everything that my friends and this world esteemed; premarital sex with multiple partners, drugs and alcohol, partying, and being the stereotypical "bad boy" was praised among my high school peers. The draw of the world was more enticing then the image of God that was presented to me by the religious system that I witnessed growing up.

However, after high school the parties got crazier and my addictions grew worse. My hedonistic tendencies drove me to places I never imagined I would go. I tried drugs and hurt people in ways I swore I never would. My incessant reckless behavior brought trouble to my doorstep time and time again. Sin took me further than I wanted to go and made me pay a price higher than I was willing to pay. It promised me satisfaction and failed to deliver all it promised. Unfortunately, I had to learn the hard way. Looking back now, the Lord has shown me the times that His hand of protection was over me, preserving my life. And there were other times He allowed me to eat the fruit of my perverse ways, revealing the consequences of living in darkness. I am truly grateful to Him for not allowing me to get away with *all* of my stupidity. Seeing my pre-Christ days with a new lens showed me how merciful God was in letting me come to the end of myself.

I spiraled into a depression. I tried more drugs, friends, girls, money, etc., but it was wasted time and energy. Happiness couldn't be found in a pill, a pint, green paper (money), or a person. Every time I fell helplessly short, still searching for someone or something to cure my internal disease. Slowly but surely, I was warming up to the idea of seeking God for help. My family was urged by Holy Spirit to pray more intensely than ever before because they sensed my breakthrough was near. They claimed me day and night for the kingdom of heaven and refused to be moved by what they saw in the natural. "For we live by faith, not by sight (2 Corinthians 5:7 NIV). I'd sit in my room, open my Bible, and the Scriptures began to intrigue me like never before. But satan was not pleased with my heart opening like a budding flower to the Spirit's prodding, and so, at the same time that my heart was opening to the Lord, suicidal thoughts started to plague my mind. The kingdom of darkness was warring hard to destroy me anyway it could.

"The thief comes only to steal and kill and destroy" (John 10:10). This continued until one fateful afternoon that I will never forget. On that day, when I couldn't bear the battle any longer, I came to approach God as my last resort.

I was alone in my room, *or at least I thought I was.* I began to pray to God with desperation. Tears were running down my face and my heart was bare before Him. With the only ounce of strength I could muster, my lips uttered to Him, "Change me God, I need You. Reveal Yourself to me." I grabbed my Bible and the first book I opened up to was the prophet Jeremiah. My eyes locked in on chapter 31 verse 16, which says, "'Restrain your voice from weeping and your eyes from tears; for your work will be rewarded,' declares the Lord. 'They will return from the land of the enemy.' "

Suddenly, like a mighty rushing wind, I felt the power and glory of His presence all around me. Instantly, my heart was consumed with His love and chills ran down my spine from His touch. My heavenly Father's arms wrapped me with His warm, accepting embrace. All at once my restlessness vanished and I was finally at ease. He calmed me and gave me a peace unlike any other; a peace the world never gave. I never felt anything so beautiful, so pure, and so powerful in my whole life. He restored my ability to experience the glory of His presence that I was always destined to know. My heart was so utterly undone that living life as usual was no longer an option. Not only did my senses awaken to feel Him, but also I heard the small, yet firm voice of Holy Spirit within me. *"You are My son, and I have plans for your life."* Those words shot through me like a lightning bolt, yet they brought such a peaceful calm to my once unsettled and anxious soul.

Years later, my mother told me that when she was seeking comfort from God during my "rebel years" the Lord gave her Jeremiah 31:16 as a promise Scripture about my salvation. How amazing is our heavenly Father for using that same Scripture to bring the salvation He promised years prior to my praying mother? *The Lord is faithful to His Word.*

> *"God is not human, that He should lie, not a human being, that He should change His mind. Does He speak and then not act? Does He promise and not fulfill?"*
>
> (Numbers 23:19 NIV).

Solomon's Example

Solomon was King David's son. He took his father's place as the king of Israel after he died. He was considered the wisest man who ever lived, besides Jesus Himself. Kings and queens from around the world traveled long distances just to meet him and witness Solomon's splendor and wisdom firsthand. During his reign he spoke three thousand proverbs and his songs numbered 1,005 (1 Kings 4:32 NIV). That is quite impressive if you ask me! He may have been wise in his sayings, but unfortunately he failed to heed his owns words throughout the majority of his life. King Solomon was fourteen years old when he became king. Imagine that! At fourteen you're barely hitting puberty and trying to cover your pimples, let alone leading an entire nation in its affairs. Towards the end of his life, he penned vulnerable words that resonate throughout the ages for our benefit.

> *"I enlarged my works: I built houses **for myself**; I planted vineyards **for myself**; I made gardens and*

*parks **for myself** and I planted in them all kinds of fruit trees; I made ponds of water **for myself** from which to irrigate a forest of growing trees. I bought male and female slaves and I had home born slaves. Also, I possessed flocks and herds larger than all who preceded me in Jerusalem. Also, I collected **for myself** silver and gold and the treasures of kings and provinces. I provided **for myself** male and female singers and the pleasures of men—many concubines...my wisdom also stood by me"*

(Ecclesiastes 2:4-9).

Notice the emphasis I put on the repeated phrase "for myself." Solomon accomplished all of these things with only himself in mind. He did what was pleasing to him, not the Lord. By seeking his own pleasure, instead of seeking what would please God's heart, he felt the weighty repercussions of his choices. There's no denying the tremendous anointing and abilities given to Solomon, but his life was consumed with the wrong things. As a child, Solomon grew up in the presence of God and he witnessed his father's radical devotion to the Lord firsthand. As a result, he was familiar with the move of God, *but didn't know the rhythms of His heart. He was able to operate in the anointing of the Spirit but didn't intimately know the love of God for himself.* What was King Solomon's conclusion in it all?

"All that my eyes desired I did not refuse them. I did not withhold my heart from any pleasure...and behold all was vanity and striving after wind and there was no profit under the sun"

(Ecclesiastes 2:10-11).

At the end of the day, when all was said and done, he came to a realization—much like mine—that all of his self-seeking was for nothing. The book of Ecclesiastes was written towards the end of Solomon's life and most of it can sound pretty miserable. It's the story of a man who had it all and still couldn't find true happiness. By the end of his life, he came to a strong conclusion. "The conclusion, when all has been heard, is: fear God and keep His commandments, because this applies to every person" (Ecclesiastes 12:13).

More cars, bigger houses, the latest technology, a hot spouse, having a vacation home in Hawaii, or even having a large, dynamic ministry cannot bring you the peace and satisfaction your soul longs for. *Only Jesus can.* It doesn't come through living life with only your own interests in mind, but seeking the interests of Him who is worthy. As the church moves from self-centered to Christ-centered, she will truly shine as the radiant and spotless bride that Jesus dreamed of in His heart from eternity past.

David's Example

King David was a whole different story from his son, Solomon. He was by no means perfect; he definitely had his fair share of failures— massive blunders if you will. But the huge difference between him and his son was he was a man after God's own heart. While Solomon's main focus was the inferior pleasures of sin, David was enraptured and captivated by the superior pleasures of God's immeasurable love towards him.

"Here's one thing I crave from God, the one thing I seek above all else: I want the privilege of living with

Him, every moment in His house, finding the sweet loveliness of His face; filled with awe, delighting in His glory and grace"

(Psalm 27:4 TPT).

"My soul yearns, even faints, for the courts of the Lord; my heart and my flesh cry out for the living God"

(Psalm 84:2 NIV).

These are only a few of King David's numerous verses of adoration and desire towards the Lord. All throughout the Psalms you see David's passion bleeding through the pages. David was adorned with riches, glory and fame but he always kept his relationship with God central—in its proper place. The world's riches were his, but that wasn't the source of his bliss, they were the benefits of his faithfulness. God's presence was the joy of David's life. He craved intimacy with God more than anything this world could offer him.

The presence of God is the pleasure we are created to indulge. If you have one too many mixed drinks at the bar, the bartender will cut you off, but God will never cut you off from drinking in His presence till your heart's content. When you taste and see that God is good, you lose the taste for things of the world. When you're love-drunk on God's Spirit, you say a determined *no* to the spirits that try to adamantly allure you into their entrapments. The passing pleasures of sin fade away the more you are filled with awe by the loveliness of Jesus' face. A fascinating truth is that in the Hebrew language there is no such word for our word *presence* that refers to God's presence. Every time you see this word used in the Old Testament, it can be best-translated "face," as in *God's face*. From this angle, we can now see the true interpretation of Psalm 16:11, "*In His face there is fullness of joy.*" Like Moses, in Exodus 33, he's described as a friend of God, speaking with Him *face-to-face*. Do you want to see God like Moses did? Do you want to know the affections of the Lord as keenly as David? The good news is that even greater supernatural dimensions are available to you because of the finished work of Christ and His indwelling Spirit within you.

True Vs. Counterfeit

A few years back, some friends and I heard of an outpouring of the Spirit taking place at a ministry school a few states away. Excited, we all packed into two cars and headed out for the week. The memory is still so vivid to me that it feels like yesterday. I'll never forget the feelings that surged through me for the first time as I walked into the room where the meetings were being held. Without wasting any time, I jumped right into worship, anticipating God to move powerfully in our midst.

The next thing I knew, the Spirit of God crashed in on me. I was drenched from head to foot with His presence. The presence was so thick that my body felt wet even though it wasn't. The atmosphere was charged with the frequency of heaven. The thoughts that ran through my mind during this encounter were, *I feel high right now, I feel like I'm on ecstasy, except it's pure, holy and full of light.*"

Ecstasy is a popular club drug often referred to as the "love pill." The reason for this title is because it heightens your perception of sound and light and amplifies sensations when someone touches or caresses you. As I was in the presence of God, the spirit of revelation opened my eyes to the strategies of satan to steal, kill, and destroy God's children. The Lord told me, "Satan has counterfeited My glory, by creating drugs to hook My beloved ones on a false 'glory' that leaves them broken and begging for more. He hooks them on the false and turns theirs hearts from the truth." Hearing those words from the mouth of God broke my heart for what breaks His. If the world only knew what they could have in God, they'd drop their endless pursuits of carnal pleasure and fall down at His throne of mercy and grace!

Today, God is reconciling satan's devious plans and turning drug addicts and alcoholics into some of the most anointed, sensitive, and devoted warriors in His kingdom. These devoted ones will take up the ministry of Jesus and destroy the works of the devil. Those who tripped out on hallucinogenic drugs are now being welcomed into the seer realm where they encounter visions from above and strategies of God for future events. Others who were "ecstasy heads" are now being absolutely undone by the pleasures from above and sharing this "heavenly love" with their friends, families, and strangers. The devil saw the specific anointing on them from birth and appealed to its propensity by offering the counterfeit. The Lord is restoring its purity and releasing sons and daughters in the supernatural ministry of Jesus to become ministers of reconciliation on the earth!

The Key of Surrender

The pathway to experiencing the divine pleasures of God's presence is a yielded heart. Jesus clearly stated in the gospel of John, "He who loves his life loses it, and he who hates his life in this world will keep it to life eternal" (John 12:25). Each one of us has bought into a false identity and built a life for ourselves that doesn't make sense according to God's sacred plan. When we lay our dreams and ambitions at the feet of our everlasting Father, He begins to unveil to us who we truly are in light of who He created us to be. And as this unveiling takes place, the blinders of the self-made person, American dream propaganda, and the vanity of pursuing success as the focal point of life suddenly lose their appeal. Seeing your true self in the eyes of the One who placed the stars in the sky will absolutely revolutionize the way you do life.

Surrender is our access into the ecstasy of God's unfathomable love. Surrender isn't just a onetime occasion; *it's a lifestyle for the believer.* It's the daily yielding of our lives and affections to our extraordinary King of glory. Joy, inexpressible and full of glory is the outcome of genuine surrender. Tragically, many believers are living far below their inheritance because they haven't stepped down from the position of "lord" in the affairs of their life.

The spirit of this world is the spirit of selfishness. The sinful nature is self-centered and self-seeking at its very core. Living for self is death, while living for Christ is life and peace. Yet, as a believer you've now become a partaker of God's divine nature (2 Peter 1:4) and the love of Christ has been poured out in your heart by the Holy Spirit (Romans 5:5). Therefore, the generous, selfless, other-giving love of God is now at work, kicking out all of your selfish tendencies as you surrender them into His loving hands. The fact of the matter is, *life is not about you…it's about Him.* Coming to grips with the revelation of absolute dependence on Him, will infuse your life with presence and power. Dependency is vital for kingdom development. Our heavenly Father reveals Himself to the child-like, not the "know it all."

God is longing for radical ones to be today's norm in the church. Radical, in fact, is normative Christianity from God's vantage point. All it takes is one taste and you won't want anything less than God's best for you. You'll kiss the American dream goodbye when you realize that the One who spoke the cosmos into existence created you, adores you, and calls you by name. Lovers of His presence believe in Him and obey Him, and it's not burdensome in the least (1 John 5:3).

How can serving your Savior and King be a burden? It's a supreme privilege and outstanding delight! Cherish every moment and drink in every touch. Jumping into the ocean of the fullness of God is a threat to the comfortable life you've created for yourself. The days of predictability and having it all figured out are over. All other lovers must come down. Yielded ones arise! Saints whose hearts are surrendered to Almighty God—take your rightful place! Sleepy sons and daughters, lulled into slumber by the passing pleasures of this world—wake up!

> "The realm of pleasure belongs squarely in God's camp. While God has surely granted us physical pleasures, emotional pleasures and mental pleasures, the most profound pleasures are spiritual in nature."
>
> —Mike Bickle[3]

Chapter 3

The High Call

"I count everything as loss compared to the possession of the priceless privilege (the overwhelming preciousness, the surpassing worth, and supreme advantage) of knowing Christ Jesus my Lord"
(Philippians 3:8 AMP).

The way of His presence is heart-to-heart, face-to-face, intimacy with Jesus. Some believers are married to traditions and religion, while Jesus is yearning for close intimate relationship with His bride—the church. Heidi Baker hit the nail directly on the head in teaching that *all fruitfulness flows from intimacy*. Everyone wants fruit, but many don't prioritize getting closer to Jesus as the pursuit of their lives. Moses spoke with the Lord face-to-face, and there is an even greater glory available to those who will draw near to the Lord today (2 Corinthians 3:7-11).

Eternal Life

Our primary purpose in life is intimacy with God. Our secondary purpose is the calling placed on our lives to make an impact in this world by the power of the Holy Spirit. Both are vitally important. Both must work together side by side. If you're keeping the main thing the main thing, then your secondary calling will function properly and powerfully as the Lord has intended. Seeking power to the neglect of relationship will eventually come to bite you—and that's not a risk you should be willing to take. Many healing revivalists in the past have fallen victim this same imbalance and reaped the painful consequences. *God's Generals* is a series of books by Roberts Liardon that shares stories of the successes and failures of men and women of God who have gone before us. I strongly recommend these books to anyone who feels a strong call to full-time ministry. It reveals the good, the bad, and the ugly in the personal lives of those who were used tremendously by the Lord in their time.

The phrase *eternal life* is one that is often misunderstood. Many believers hear the words *eternal life* and solely think of heaven and hell. On the contrary, eternal life is the very reason Jesus came and died for us. Eternal life is the gift of God. "For the wages of sin is death, but the free gift of God is eternal life in Christ Jesus our Lord" (Romans 6:23). The church often uses the words *eternal life*, and rightfully so—but fails to accurately define it. Jesus made no such mistake. He said, "This is eternal life, that they may know You, the only true God, and Jesus Christ whom You have sent" (John 17:3).

Friend, eternal life is to know God and Jesus Christ, who was sent to become the substitute for your sins. Jesus took your place, carried your sin, and broke down the barrier of separation between you and God. You can now approach the Lord's presence with outrageous boldness! His presence has been restored to you. Sin's separation has been abolished and you can now fellowship with your heavenly Father again. When you say the word *eternity*, most people just think of heaven and hell, when the reality of eternity is all about knowing Him, *here and now*, not just some far-off day in heaven.

The Main Thing

Eternal significance is calculated by the depth of our intimacy with God. The book of Daniel reveals that those who know their God will display strength and take action (Daniel 11:32). It's impossible to do great exploits without first intimately knowing God. His Spirit is the strength of our lives. Without Him and His strength we're doomed to fail. Doing great exploits shouldn't be your focus until you learn to sit at His feet and listen to the words that flow from His mouth. You shouldn't concentrate all your time and energy on fulfilling the Great Commission without first submitting your heart to the process of knowing the God of the Great Commission. Sadly, ministers and believers alike are living off of fumes because intimacy isn't the fuel that's keeping their spiritual engine running.

In the following chapter, the prophet Daniel speaks of the day when Jesus comes back for His bride and the dead are raised in eternal resurrection and taken to their heavenly homes.

> *"And at that time your people, everyone who is found written in the book, will be rescued. Many of those who sleep in the dust of the ground will awake, these to everlasting life, but the others to disgrace and everlasting contempt.*
>
> ***Those who have insight will shine brightly like the brightness of the expanse of heaven, and those who lead the many to righteousness, like the stars forever and ever"***
>
> (Daniel 12:1-3).

As we can see from the verse in bold the character qualities of the saints who will rise with Christ on the glorious day of His coming are *heavenly insight* and *passion for the lost.* For both of these qualities to be fleshed out through us, it's imperative that we grow in the love of God. Let's take a deeper look at this. For starters, those who seek God, *find God.* Also, those who find Him are given access into the revelations that flow from His lips. Therefore, *intimacy is the pathway into heavenly insight.* On top of that, those who know the Lord intimately are those who are compelled to reach the lost. It's impossible to burn for the lost without first being introduced to the burning heart of God that is inflamed for those who are perishing. As we can see, intimacy also is the road to a life poured out for the lost. When you love Jesus, you can't help but share the revelations He's given you of the gospel with the world at large. His love begins to ooze from your entire being. His love is uncontainable!

Jesus came first and foremost to restore our union with God. It's your connection with the Spirit of God—through the love and romance of the gospel—that fuels you to accomplish mighty exploits in His name. Intimacy isn't a means to a greater end—it's the crux of the gospel. Nothing else works without intimacy.

Forsaking All to Know Him

My encounter with Christ is the reason for my passion to reach the world with the gospel. The reality that I can know Him more, hear His voice, experience His presence, and connect heart-to-heart with Him is the motivation of my life. Christianity without the presence of Christ is religion. Going through the motions sustained in the flesh, without the empowerment of His Spirit is religion. I don't even want to imagine being a Christian without His presence. Vanity of vanities!

I wouldn't want to do what I do if it wasn't for Immanuel "God with us." The very fact that I'm not following Jesus from a distance, but that He is with me every step of the way makes the Great Commission worth pursuing. My passion is being fueled by divine intimacy, compelling me to go where others wouldn't dare go and step out in ways that make others cringe! That's the effect of His life-giving presence.

"For woe is me if I don't preach the gospel"
(1 Corinthians 9:16).

Paul, the great apostle of God's grace, was consumed with holy zeal and unrestrained enthusiasm to see the nations come into faith. He was no longer motivated by legalism and the traditions of men—but driven by the Spirit of the living God working mightily within him.

Of all people for God to choose to be a herald of the good news of salvation, He chose Paul—an aggressive and violent persecutor of the first church. For the majority of his life, Paul was praised for his strict adherence to the Law of Moses and the traditions of the Jews. Nonetheless, once he encountered the person of Jesus in that one pivotal Damascus Road encounter, everything drastically changed. From that time onward, Christ became his *holy obsession*— his reason for living. Check out these verses in the Amplified Bible and pay close attention to the language used in the text.

*"But whatever former things were gains to me…these things [once regarded as advancements in merit] I have come to consider as loss [absolutely worthless] for the sake of Christ [and the purpose which He has given my life]. But more than that, **I count everything as loss compared to the priceless privilege and supreme advantage of knowing Christ Jesus my Lord [and of growing more deeply and thoroughly acquainted with Him—a joy unequaled]. For His sake I have lost everything, and I consider it all garbage, so that I may gain Christ…**And this, so that I may know Him [experientially, becoming more thoroughly acquainted with Him, understanding the remarkable wonders of His Person more completely]"*

(Philippians 3:7-10 AMP).

Amazing! The great apostle counted all things loss for the priceless privilege and supreme advantage of knowing Jesus. Nothing meant more to him than growing in his relationship with the Lord. His resume was fully loaded and his zeal surpassed those of his time. He was widely recognized for his courage, obedience, and dedication to God. Once he encountered Jesus Christ, none of those accomplishments and badges of honor mattered anymore. In fact, he considered his resume and successes absolute garbage in comparison to getting closer to Jesus Christ. Check this verse out where Paul continues:

"Not that I have already obtained it…or have already been made perfect, but I actively press on so that I may take hold of that [perfection] for which

Christ Jesus took hold of me and made me His own. Brothers and sisters, I do not consider that I have made it my own yet; but one thing I do: forgetting what lies behind and reaching forward to what lies ahead, **I press on toward the goal to win the [heavenly] prize of the upward call of God in Christ Jesus"**

(Philippians 3:12-14 AMP).

From this passage we can see that the apostle Paul is pressing on toward the goal of obtaining the prize of the upward call of God in Christ Jesus. In Bible school we'd often be encouraged to seek and pursue the high calling of the Lord. A lot of the time, it seemed as though the high calling was referring to winning souls and doing the work of the ministry. We'd hear stories of men like Smith Wigglesworth, John G. Lake, Gordon Lindsay, and others who operated in the miraculous. So, what is this upward call of God that the apostle is speaking about? Is it having a miracle ministry? What about even living a life absorbed in the works of the kingdom of God? All of these things are valid and essential, but they are *the fruit*, not *the root*.

Over the years, I've come to understand that the apostle Paul here wasn't talking about his miracles and the number of people converted because of his preaching. The context of this passage is forsaking everything to attain closeness and a more intimate revelation-knowledge of our Lord Jesus Christ. He was the goal of this great apostle's life, and He must be the goal of ours too! People aren't looking for more intellectual knowledge or facts to cling to. If they were, they could apply to a university or one of the many cemetery-like seminaries out there to feed their lust for knowledge. The world is searching for something tangible and real. When your words have been formed in the secret place with Jesus they are spirit and life. In the same way that children are conceived through the intimacy of a man and woman, spiritual fruit is the outcome of our intimacy with the Lord. The only way to gain fruit that both remains and matters on the other side of eternity is to abide in His love (John 15:5). Revival in the secret place will lead to revival in the public place.

Encountering Jesus radically revolutionizes everything. You can never be the same again. What is it about this Jesus that inspires people from all walks of life to drop their earthly pursuits and live for eternal realities? What is it about this Jesus that compels ordinary people to move to remote parts of the world, live far below their previous means, and lay down their lives for a group of people they've never met before? The life of faith makes no sense to the carnal mind. But *where there is love, no sacrifice is too great.* In fact, sacrifice doesn't even feel like sacrifice when your reward is eternal love. There's something about this Jesus that captivates our hearts to such a degree that nothing seems to make sense anymore without wholehearted abandonment to His will and ways!

Look at how His disciples responded to Him when they encountered Him, as illustrated in the Gospels:

> *"Now as Jesus was walking by the Sea of Galilee, He saw two brothers, Simon who was called Peter, and Andrew his brother, casting a net into the sea; for they were fishermen. And He said to them, 'Follow Me, and I will make you fishers of men.'*

Immediately they left their nets and followed Him.
Going on from there He saw two other brothers,
James the son of Zebedee, and John his brother, in
the boat with Zebedee their father, mending their
nets; and He called them. **Immediately they left the**
boat and their father, and followed Him."

(Matthew 4:18-22)

"*Afterward, Jesus went out and looked for a man*
named Matthew. He found him sitting at his tax
booth, for he was a tax collector. Jesus said to him,
'be my disciple and follow Me.' **That very moment,**
Matthew got up, left every behind, and followed
Him."

(Luke 5:27-28 TPT)

These men instinctively knew their lives were meant for more than the nine-to-five, daily grind lifestyle they were living. Their seeking hearts were enraptured and attracted to this Jesus, who is altogether lovely! The draw of Christ, His pursuit, His everlasting beauty charms us and enchants us to the point where nothing can hold a match to Him! That's the power of His presence. That's the beauty of who He is. None can compare! Nothing else will do. Following Him was worth more than the security a career could bring them. Jesus became the pursuit of the disciple's lives. *What's your main pursuit?*

If you've never heard the voice of God, felt His life-giving presence, or encountered Him in such a way that it transformed you from the inside out, reach out to Him today. He wants intimacy with you, even more than you want it with

Him. He's placed those desires within you— now draw near to Him. In return, He promises to draw near to you.

Israel's Largest Blunder

In the book of Exodus, Israel was enslaved to Egypt and cried out to the Lord for deliverance from their oppressors. In response to their earnest prayer of help, the Lord crashed in to deliver them with His mighty hand. God used Moses and Aaron to spearhead this freedom movement. From Egypt into the wilderness, the Lord did not personally interact with the children of Israel Himself. Instead, Moses was God's right-hand man who delivered the Lord's messages to the people.

> *"The Lord also said to Moses, 'Go to the people and consecrate them today and tomorrow* [that is, prepare them for My sacred purpose], *and have them wash their clothes and be ready by the third day, because on the third day the Lord will come down on Mount Sinai* [in the cloud] *in the sight of all the people' "*
>
> (Exodus 19:10-11).

The Lord who delivered them from Egypt with a mighty arm is now going to *come down* and *reveal Himself.* Isn't that amazing? *God is coming down to them.* He truly is the God who stoops down to His people and makes Himself known. He doesn't demand us to climb our way up to Him—He knows the impossibility of such a venture. Instead, in His compassion and tender mercies He comes down to Israel. But how did they respond on this glorious day of meeting?

"All the people perceived the thunder and the lightning flashes and the sound of the trumpet and the mountain smoking; and when the people saw it, **they trembled and stood at a distance.** *Then they said to Moses, 'Speak to us yourself and we will listen; but let not God speak to us, or we will die.'...So the people stood at a distance, while Moses approached the thick cloud where God was"*

(Exodus 20:18-21).

God drew near to them, *and they stood at a distance from Him.* They actually cried out for a mediator over having personal communication with the living God. Israel demanded law over relationship when they told Moses, "Speak to us yourself...but let not God speak with us." In the same way that God came down to the Israelites to appear to them in the wilderness, two thousand years ago, God broke into the natural realm and came down to His beloved creation through the Person of Jesus Christ. Thousands of years after the Exodus, did Israel respond any differently to the glory of God being revealed in their midst? Sadly, the answer is no. Instead of receiving Him, they accused Him of being demonic, beat Him, ripped His back to shreds, imbedded a crown of thorns in His forehead, and hung Him to die naked on the cross in utter humiliation and shame. *And they did it in the name of God!*

When Israel chose the Law over God, they chose religion over relationship. They wanted commands over face-to-face communion. Did you know that it's possible to be a born again, Spirit-filled believer, and yet in your heart live at a distance with God? Jesus said it Himself, "These people honor me with their lips, but their hearts are far from me" (Matthew 15:8 NIV). Did you know you could also be a born again, Spirit-filled believer, and—like Israel—die in the wilderness before ever inheriting the Promised Land prepared for you to enter? How many dreams have been aborted among God's people? How many promises left unfulfilled?

He won't force Himself upon you, beloved. He won't grab you by the neck and command you to be His friend. If you want religion, you can have religion. If you prefer to be a mere acquaintance of God instead of a personal friend— the choice is yours. There is no condemnation for you, but you will miss out on the beauty of knowing Him and the glory of all you've been destined to experience. My advice: don't settle for shallow waters but fully immerse yourself in the ocean of the fullness of God.

Some years ago, a friend and I used to set aside time to pray and seek God together. My friend was praying out loud and pacing around the room, while I was praying in tongues to myself. Suddenly, the Holy Spirit whispered to me, "Your friend has a word for you." Patiently, I waited to see if I heard correctly from the Lord. A few minutes passed before he spun around and began to prophesy, "Michael, the Lord showed me a vision of an ocean that was vast, wide, and spectacular beyond compare. The ocean represents the depths of revelation and grace that's available to you. The Lord says that you've been dipping your toes in the water, splashing around in the shallow end, but He's calling you to come deeper and fully submerge yourself in the ocean of all that He is!" At first, I was taken back because I considered myself to be a radical seeker of God. I didn't think I was only splashing around in the shallow end. I took a moment to think about it. "If I'm experiencing His love and presence now, and this is only the shallow stuff, then there must be so much more that God wants to reveal to me!" I let go of my foolish pride and chose to say *yes* to the Lord in going deeper into the multi-faceted dimensions of His revelation-light and glory. Will you answer the same call? Don't settle for ankle deep, knee deep or ever waist deep. Fully immerse yourself in the fullness of His glorious presence!

The Prevalence of Religion

The church is filled with believers who claim His name, *yet they don't actually know Him.* My heart breaks over this reality. They sing about being friends with God, but their hearts are distant from Him, completely disengaged. The Israelites possessed a form of godliness, but no heart-to-heart connection with the Lord. Today, this same religiosity engrosses God's people. The reason I believe religion is so prevalent in the church is because people don't want to heed the words of Christ. Many want to live their own lives and chase their own dreams without being tampered with by anyone—even Jesus. Sadly, the church is swarming with people who want to put on a facade, smiling big and wide and saying all the right Christian words while holding on tight to their own ways of living.

Out of the heart flow all the issues of life. Religion doesn't have the power to penetrate the heart, and that's why it appeals to the masses. A false assurance takes the place of genuine salvation and truth. Religious people may say, "If I go to church most Sundays, if my good outweighs my bad when I die, if I treat others like I'd want to be treated, if I don't commit any atrocious sins (insert whatever sin you deem the worst), then all is well and I'm okay with God." All of these mindsets are lies from the enemy and are anti-gospel to the very root. Religion's power is only dismantled through *encountering the love of Jesus.* The love of God softens the hardest hearts, breaks the strongest chains, and has the power to infuse unshakable passion into His slumbering bride.

I'd be bold enough to say that religion is the foulest sin in the eyes of God above all else. As you read through the gospels, you see an unchanging theme: Jesus offers forgiveness and healing to the worst of sinners, and He strongly corrects those of the religious elite who esteem themselves higher than others. I can't tell you how many beautiful people I've met who've shared their horror stories of going to a church to seek help in desperate times. Sadly, all they received was judgment from so-called "believers." I believe that God's heart is broken over the individuals who come seeking truth and guidance from churches all over the world; and find nothing but the judgmental eyes of modern-day Pharisees. All they get are stones being thrown at them for their sinful lifestyles. Religion is the strongest bondage there is, because those trapped in its grip don't even know they are bound.

In Exodus 20, the Israelites drew back, but Moses unreservedly approached the thick cloud where God was. I want to be like Moses and speak with God face-to-face. I want to boldly and tenaciously approach the thick cloud of glory where God dwells. I never want to pull away from the nearness of God into self-reliance and religious obligations.

An Army of Lovers

Five years ago I had a vision where I saw Jesus sitting on His throne far off in the distance. *From His throne,* an army of believers were marching together in unison with their faces set like flint on the Lord's will and work. The significance of this vision is two-fold:

First, the warriors of God were marching *from* His throne room. The throne room is a place of *intimacy.* In Christ, we're now seated in His throne room in the heavenly places (Ephesians 2:6). There; you have full access to commune with Him *in person.* That infers that these warriors are a presence-driven people, not a purpose-driven people. Purpose is wonderful, but our first purpose in life is to know Him intimately.

Second, because they were coming forth from the throne room, there is a divine commissioning involved. Once you become intimately relational with the Lord, He begins to reveal to you the burdens of His heart and your true purpose in Him. You must then submit yourself to the training that is required and the equipping that is necessary to best function in your area of calling—and the mission comes later. Workers burn out, but lovers burn on and on and on. When you become a lover of His presence, He becomes your source and sustaining power in all things.

The Lord isn't raising up a passive or lethargic generation. His lovers are anointed to get more done than those who strive according to the flesh. This is the Lord's generation of warriors who are arising around the globe with dogged determination to continually dwell in the glory of His presence. These warriors consider it sheer joy to lay down their lives for the sake of the gospel. Today's co-laborers must also be bridal lovers. First and foremost, and of upmost importance, *will you answer this call to divine intimacy?* There is no higher call. The invitation has been extended, and it's up to you to respond.

Child of God, the King of all kings and Lord of all lords has branded you with a heavenly calling that far exceeds what you are able to accomplish in your own skills, ideas and abilities. Once you answer the call to intimacy, He begins to reveal destiny. It's not a question of being called or not. The real question is, *will you answer the call?* Lovers don't give God conditions or ultimatums. As long as His presence is with you, nothing else should matter!

Ascribe value and worth to Jesus by prioritizing His presence. He longs to pour His presence upon all who draw near to Him with sincerity of heart and full assurance of faith. The more you see Him, the more you'll love Him. The closer you get to His all-consuming flame of love, the more your heart will burn for Him and the world around you.

"Were not our hearts burning within us while He was speaking to us on the road, while He was explaining the Scriptures to us?"

(Luke 24:32).

Chapter 4
Is Jesus Enough?

*"Then he said to Him, 'If Your presence does not go
with us, do not lead us up from here'"*

(Exodus 33:15).

When I accepted Christ, He became the focal point and
driving force of my life. All I wanted was more of Him. His
love swept me off my feet and my sole ambition was to
remain wide-eyed and mystified in His holy presence.

Throughout the day my spiritual eyes were opened to
see His fingerprints and activity all around me. In my
prayer time He'd show me pictures and visions. One
specifically that changed everything, happened only a few
weeks into my new life in Christ. While I laid in bed the
Lord showed me a vision of myself sitting with a random
individual who I couldn't quite distinguish. Eventually, that
person stood up and left, and two others came to replace
him. Following suit, those two left and three others walked
up to sit with me. Then suddenly, the vision faded to black
and another vision instantly appeared. I saw a sea of faces
so vast and numerous that I couldn't see beyond them. It
was the largest crowd I have ever seen, and immediately I
heard the still small voice of the Lord, *"Son, first I will have
you speak to few, then I will have you speak to many."*

This was my "follow Me" moment. I knew right then and
there that God created me in my mother's womb with
purpose. From then on, I began my quest of pursuing this
calling with all my heart.

As a young, naïve Christian I was hoping that this dream's fulfillment would be right around the corner. I wanted to go and preach to the multitudes and I didn't want to wait! At night when I laid my head on my pillow, I would envision these things unfolding before my eyes. Little did I know that I was in the essential process of preparation and God wasn't in as big of a hurry as I was. Trusting God, I still held tightly to that vision, refusing to become discouraged.

While attending Bible school, a missionary from Argentina visited and preached about the honor of knowing Christ. He was preaching boldly that we should forsake everything, even our own desires. I remember having a hard time with that message. Everyone in the auditorium exuberantly raised their hands to forsake it all, and I didn't feel comfortable joining the party. The Lord was dealing with a very sensitive and tender issue of my heart.

The Lord then asked me, "Son, what would happen if that dream I gave you about preaching to the multitudes never came to fruition? *Am I enough for you?*" It was as though a dagger was pushed into my chest. I didn't understand why God would ask such a thing. He gave me the vision, so why would he ask me to die to it? After hours of pondering and praying, I came to a place of understanding and trust. I came to believe that God wasn't taking the dream away from me— He was sifting and purifying my intentions. Jesus didn't want to compete with the calling He placed on my life and He won't compete with yours either.

The Holy Spirit is a blazing fire of love, and a vital part of His job description is to purify our intentions and motives until they brilliantly reflect the nature of Christ. He'll highlight these areas of intention not to condemn us—*but to free us.* Never despise the Lord's correction. Embrace His Fatherhood. He corrects and challenges every child He receives. It's for your good, beloved of God.

Later on that year I went on my first mission trip to Thailand, Laos, and Malaysia. A pastor who was doing a tremendous work in the mountains of Malaysia took our team to minister to the various churches he had planted among former Muslims in the area. I'll never forget the sweet and tangible presence of God that filled our times of worship. Guitars were missing strings, little girls were singing out of tune and it was a hundred degrees outside, but the Lord's presence was so rich and full among us that I could hardly stand up. There were no fog machines, fancy lights, electric guitars, or microphones—but Jesus was there in the midst of His people, highly enthroned upon the praises of His Malaysian bride. A crippled man who was practically skin and bones lifted his hands to heaven with tears streaming down his face, worshiping the one true God with all his heart, mind, and strength. Poverty-stricken people who were in desperate need came together to praise and worship their King who loves and saved them.

Moments like this one will change you forever. Especially when all you've known is western Christianity. No threat of persecution looms over our heads. No lack for basic necessities concerns many of us living in America. Hospitals and doctor's offices are a few miles away whenever we need them. But these people struggle and suffer every day just for claiming the name of Christ. Then

51

the Lord took out His pruning shears and held nothing back by asking me a set of heart wrenching questions. "Would you be okay if I raised you up to be a missionary in a place like this, among a people of this nature? How about living here in the mountains pouring out your life for the sake of My dear ones in these remote villages? Would you be okay with never holding a microphone, writing a book, or being famous for what you do? *Am I enough for you?*"

To say the least, I was shocked and shaken to the core of my being. Those words were the Lord's pruning shears to bring forth more fruit in me. The Lord prunes those whom He loves. Pruning causes more fruit to spring up from within us. It's His Word that cleanses and purifies us of attitudes, intentions and beliefs that hinder the fullness of His love and plan from being felt and experienced.

Cut to the core, I confronted the idolatry of self-glorification that I craved. Upon examining my heart I came to the truest and only conclusion I could come to. I told Him, "Of course Lord. I would live in obscurity, pouring out my life for You and Your kids. You love me and that's all that matters!" When you give Jesus access into every area of your heart, both the good and bad, you set yourself up for serious spiritual transformation. *Will you let the Lord sift through your heart's motives to fashion more of His Son's image in you?*

The Promiser

Now let's take a look at men and women who are known for their radical devotion to the Lord. In the Old Testament, Abraham was considered righteous in the eyes of God even before Christ came to die for the sins of the world. His confident trust foreshadowed the faith that new covenant believers would possess in God today. As the story goes, the Lord promised Abraham a son, even though his wife was barren and beyond the age of child bearing. Abraham's wife finally conceived after quite some time and they gave birth to a boy named Isaac. One day God appeared to Abraham and told him,

> *"Take your son, your only son, whom you love— Isaac—and go to the region of Moriah. Sacrifice him there as a burnt offering on a mountain I will show you"*
>
> (Genesis 22:2 NIV).

Abraham didn't argue with God after receiving this command. He could have pointed out how Isaac was his miracle baby. He could have reminded the Lord (like He needed reminding) that Isaac was a manifestation of the Lord's promise to him. It was God's hand that made all of these things happen; now He's asking for Isaac to be offered as a sacrifice? Nonetheless, Abraham didn't say a peep. He woke up bright and early, packed his belongings, and took Isaac with him on this three- day trek to the region of Moriah. Numerous elements are at work here in this story but I want to hone in on one specific detail—the heart of Abraham. God was testing Abraham's heart to see if he truly feared Him. *The Lord wanted to see if Abraham loved the promise (Isaac, his son) more than he loved his God who gave the promise.* When all was said and done, God never wanted Isaac sacrificed (he wasn't, God provided the sacrifice)—He wanted to test the condition and posture of Abraham's heart.

Abraham was considered a friend of God in the Scriptures. Why? He was confident in God's heart and integrity because he knew Him personally and intimately. The Bible says Abraham trusted that God would either provide a sacrifice Himself (Genesis 22:8), or He would raise his son from the dead (Hebrews 11:19). When all is said and done, Abraham was the kind of man who loved God above all. He loved God when the fulfillment of the promise seemed bleak, and he sought God when he was living in the blessing. To this day, Abraham is considered the father of our faith.

It's one thing to seek God when life is difficult; it's another thing entirely to seek God when you're living the dream. A guest minister who was sharing at church one Sunday encouraged the people to raise their hands if they seek God more when life is hard. He seemed pretty confident that a lot of people were going to lift up their hands for that one. After that, he asked the people who tend to seek God more when life is easy to raise their hands. This time, his demeanor and tone of voice insinuated that he didn't expect many to respond to this call. The tension in the room was so thick that you could've cut it with a knife. Because it was apparent that the preacher was doing this "hand-raising" experiment to lead into his next point, the congregation had a hard time answering honestly. My heart began to break because the point he was making isn't what true friendship with God is all about. I don't only call my friends up when I need help and counsel. I don't seek my wife's attention primarily when trouble arises. If we would take the time and truly get to know God, we'd seek Him earnestly in the good times and the bad. He's our bliss, our joy, and our ever-present help in times of need.

For instance, Israel stayed true to God when trouble surrounded them, but they often forsook Him when ease set in and the blessing abounded. Even in their deliverance from Egypt, God took them *through* the wilderness to make it to the Promised Land. Why did He do that? Why couldn't they immediately inherit the land? The answer is found in Moses proclamation to Pharaoh when he pleaded with him to let God's people go. "The Lord, the God of the Hebrews, has sent me to say to you: Let my people go, so that *they may worship me in the wilderness* (Exodus 7:16 NIV). God rescued the Israelites not just to lead them to a land overflowing with insurmountable blessing, He graciously took them through the wilderness so that they could get to know Him *before* they inherited the blessings. As God's chosen people, the apple of His eye, His royal priesthood and holy nation—let's seek Him in the turbulent and triumphant times. He's worthy of our full devotion and worship.

Moses' Heart Cry

Now, I want to take a close look into the life of a few more biblical figures that paint a clear picture for us of what intimacy with the Lord is all about.

First, I want to talk about Moses. As the leader of this supernatural movement of liberation and deliverance, a lot of responsibility rested on his shoulders. Day in and day out he had to listen to the constant grumbling and complaining of God's people. He was the main judge handling everyone's disputes amongst one another. Regardless of all Moses was doing to serve the children of Israel, they continued to spurn his anointed leadership. No one wanted to get out of the wilderness and step into the Promised Land more than Moses. Despite everything, Moses cried out to the Lord, "If Your presence does not go with us, do not lead us up from here" (Exodus 33:15). That's amazing!

God then affirmed Moses by saying, *"My presence will go with you and I'll give you rest."* More than anything, Moses wanted God—even over comfort and convenience. He'd rather starve in the wilderness with God's presence then inherit a land of abundance without God's presence with him. Moses was a true lover of God. And guess what happened?

> *"Then Moses said, 'I pray You, show me Your glory!' And He said, 'I Myself will make all My goodness pass before you, and will proclaim the name of the Lord before you; and I will be gracious to whom I will be gracious, and will show compassion on whom I will show compassion.' But He said, 'You cannot see My face, for no man can see Me and live!' Then the Lord said, 'Behold, there is a place by Me, and you shall stand there on the rock; and it will come about, while My glory is passing by, that I will put you in the cleft of the rock and cover you with My hand until I have passed by. Then I will take My hand away and you shall see My back, but My face shall not be seen'"*

(Exodus 33:18-23).

I want to point out a few things from the above passage because it's filled with prophetic insight. God told Moses, "Okay, My friend, if you want to see My glory, there is a place by Me...in the cleft of the rock." The cleft rock is a type and shadow of Christ. Moses needed to be hidden in Christ before he could see the glory of God. Why? Because no mere human being can see God's glory and live to tell the story. But when you are hidden in Christ, you are more than merely a human—you are a new creation! As new creations we are supernatural children of God with the spiritual capacity to experience God's glory in an up close and personal manner. This was an Old Testament foreshadowing of a new covenant reality. Hidden in Christ, you are safe and secure to dwell permanently in the presence of our faithful Father. Another significant aspect of this invitation to Moses is that the Lord told him this place is by Him. According to Ephesians 2:6, all believers are seated in heavenly places with Christ Jesus. And where is Christ seated? He is seated at the right of His Father. Which means we are spiritually at the Father's right hand, hidden in the Son, forever in the presence of His Majesty! That's something to celebrate!

A missionary friend once asked me, "How do you get into God's presence when you pray?" I took a moment to reflect on the best possible way to answer. Then I responded, "I get into God's presence by believing that I'm already *in* His presence." We don't start outside of God and then step into Him through prayer. The starting point is in Him—your acknowledgment and prayer simply leads you into an awareness, which ushers you into an experience.

Gazing Upon Moses

*"Now Moses used to take the tent and pitch it outside the camp, a good distance from the camp, and he called it the **tent of meeting**. And everyone who sought the Lord would go out to the tent of meeting, which was outside the camp. And it came about, whenever Moses went out to the tent that all the people would arise and stand, each at the entrance of his tent, and **gaze after Moses** until he entered the tent. **Whenever Moses entered the tent**, the pillar of cloud would descend and stand at the entrance of the tent; and the Lord would speak with Moses. When all the people saw the pillar of cloud standing at the entrance of the tent, all the people would arise and worship, each at the entrance of his tent"*

(Exodus 33:7-10).

This section of Scripture is rich with revelation for us to feast upon. First, I want to point out the name *tent of meeting*. This was the place where God chose to reveal Himself to His people. They drew near to Him, and in turn He drew near to them. Here, *in that spot,* these men encountered the Lord God Almighty—Maker of the heavens and the earth. It was their place of intimate meeting with Him. You too can set up your own personal tent of meeting with the Lord. By no means does it have to be a physical tent, but a place where you lay everything at His feet in prayer and adoration. Prayer is meant to be the meeting of lovers, time spent with your Papa, and sharing life with your closest friend. Coming into prayer you must know that He is with you. He's been waiting for you to set your gaze upon Him, and Jesus is passionately singing over you, "Let me see your radiant face and hear your sweet voice. How beautiful your eyes of worship and lovely your voice in prayer" (Song of Songs 2:14 TPT).

Imagine this: Moses—the man of God, the friend of God—would draw near to the tent of meeting. All the children of Israel would stand outside of their tents and *gaze after Moses* until he reached the meeting place. Whenever Moses entered the tent, the glory cloud of the Lord would descend upon it and the voice of the Lord would speak to Moses. What a beautiful truth—when Moses came, the glory came—*the glory of God rests upon the friends of God.*

What I find interesting is that the people's focus wasn't on the Lord, but they fastened their gaze upon Moses. Today, the church falls victim to the same snare. I know people who attend church on Sunday, hear a word from their pastor, and go home to never think of God again until the following Sunday. They are dependent on their pastors and leaders for words from God and don't seek Him out for themselves.

Other believers are always devouring teaching materials, sermons, Christian living books etc., and they fail to develop and cultivate an intimate relationship with Jesus for themselves. Whenever they talk about God, they are constantly quoting other ministers sounding more like a parrot than a genuine expression of living revelation. As we speak of the Lord, it's meant to come from a vibrant, Spirit-filled revelation that we've received as a download from the Holy Spirit. When I speak with one of these people I often look them in the eye and challenge them, "Yes, what that man of God is teaching is great, but what has the Holy Spirit spoken *to you* lately?"

Saying all of this, I am by no means diminishing the role of the teacher. I'm called to be a teacher of God's Word myself and to bring the church into a greater understanding and experience in God. God will use the teacher to reveal His Word to you, but the point is never to become dependent on letting others do all the work.

The revelation these ministers are sharing—hopefully— they are receiving because they've sought God with sincerity and faith. We should do the same. Dutch Sheets powerfully articulated in his book *The Pleasure of His Company*:

> "God isn't into surrogate parenting—someone else carrying His seed of revelation for us. He wants to sow it into us *personally*, breathing His word into our hearts. Insights we receive from others through sermons and books are good and valid, but if that is the only way we receive spiritual insight, we're living far below our privileges. God isn't into artificial insemination, either— placing His seed within us without intimate relationship. Cd's, seminars and books are all good but they must not take the place of hearing from Him *personally* and *directly*...we must not be satisfied only with another's."[1]

While in the wilderness, manna would fall from heaven for the Israelites to eat, and they were forbidden to save the leftovers for the following day. Each day they had to gather fresh manna, because the leftovers would rot by morning. Likewise, as believers today, we can't live off of yesterday's manna. I don't want to survive on crumbs. We need to eat of His Word daily and be filled afresh with His Spirit.

Jesus said, "My flesh is true food and My blood is true drink." (John 6:55) He encouraged His people to eat of Him and drink of Him. The supernatural manna that fell from heaven, that sustained Israel in the wilderness—*was Jesus Christ*. He is your heavenly food. Just like your body craves earthly food, your spirit craves spiritual food.

May Jesus be your daily feast. May your eyes be fixed on Him. The people gazed at Moses, but Moses was locked in on God.

Joshua: The Lover of God

"When Moses returned to the camp, his servant Joshua, the son of Nun, a young man, would not depart from the tent"

(Exodus 33:11).

The watchful eye of the Lord searched to and fro throughout the land scouting for a man whose heart was fully devoted to Him. Joshua, the son of Nun, caught His eye. The children of Israel would draw near as Moses drew near, and leave as Moses left. But the Scripture records something so wonderful and precious in verse 11. I believe the reason the Lord wanted it here is to give us insight into the reason why God chose Joshua to lead the people into the Promised Land after Moses died. In the above verse, it reads that Moses would leave the tent of meeting, but Joshua, a young lover of God, would not depart from the tent. Joshua couldn't drag himself away from the place of communion with his God and Father. He lingered long, soaking in every drop he could. All he wanted was more of God and no one could hold him back!

Have you ever met with a close friend and ended up talking for hours and hours with that person, sharing, reminiscing, and laughing together and before you knew it, it was much later than you expected? You got so caught up with that individual that time faded away as all of your attention and focus was on that person and the conversation you shared. God is yearning for that kind of friendship with His people. Time flies when you're eating at the King's table.

There are times when I could be distracted with thousands of things, yet my spirit is being drawn by the Love of my life. In those moments, I have a choice to make—be distracted or pull away and spend quality time with my Jesus. I constantly aim to answer His call and find a private place where it can just be Him and I. *A place of meeting.* All else disappears in the face of my Love, Jesus Christ. Joshua was such a man. He was young, in love, bubbling over with passion and zeal, and God thought, *That's him! I can trust him to lead My people into the Promised Land and conquer the enemies who reside there.* When your heart is fixated on Him and His presence above all else, you become the kind of person the Lord can entrust with large missions.

In my Bible school days, we'd have a theology class before lunch at noon. The speaker would finish up and the students would rush out before the lunch line grew too long. Powerful and anointed ministers frequently came in to impart into the student body. I remember days where God's Spirit was moving so powerfully that the hungry ones didn't want to break for lunch. There would be twenty to thirty students, sometimes more depending on the day, lingering long in God's presence, receiving from His hands of mercy and love. We'd be scattered across the whole auditorium in our own world with the Lord. Some would be lying prostrate on the floor in surrender and awe. Others would be rolling around laughing in the Spirit. Some would be crying before the Lord as their tears soaked their Bible pages. Regardless of the manifestation that was taking place, these were true lovers of God—at His feet, receiving ministry from the King of kings and the Lord of lords.

At His Feet

There is a woman in Scripture who has become very dear to me over the years. I believe she perfectly displays the type of lifestyle the bride of Christ is destined to exemplify. Years ago, the Holy Spirit highlighted Mary of Bethany to me, and I've never been the same since. This woman is only mentioned three times in the gospels, but each time she's found at the same sacred place—the feet of Jesus. In Scripture, this place represents surrender and devotion.

In Luke 10, Jesus visited the home of Martha and Mary because He loved them very much (John 11:5). While Martha ran around frantically preparing everything for Jesus, Mary was in a different zone altogether. Mary was *seated at His feet,* eyes fastened upon His face, listening to the words that flowed from His mouth. While Martha anxiously tried to please Jesus with her acts of service, Mary chose the most pleasing place of all—*His feet.*

In John 11, Mary and Martha's brother (Lazarus) was sick and on the verge of death. Instead of calling the doctors, they called doctor Jesus and asked Him to pray for Lazarus. As the story goes, Jesus intentionally waited two

63

days before He began His journey and arrived late. By that time it was too late—Lazarus died. He was already in his tomb for four days. When Martha and Mary heard that Jesus was in town, Martha rushed out to speak with Him while Mary decided to stay back and nurse her heartache. In verse 28, Martha returned to Mary and told her, "The Teacher is here and is calling for you." Immediately Mary ran out to Jesus and *fell at His feet* in utter brokenness and desperation, crying out, "Lord, if You had been here, my brother would not have died!" Regardless of the season in your life, your hurts and pains, your questions and your doubts, it's necessary that you fall at His feet and get vulnerable with Jesus, like Mary. He'll take you to unimaginable places of beauty and bliss. And on top of that, He'll bring the resurrection power you need, like He did with Lazarus when he was later raised!

In the very next chapter, John 12, Jesus is again at the house of Martha, Mary, and Lazarus. They are celebrating the extraordinary miracle of Jesus bringing their brother back from death. The Bible records that Mary took a very costly perfume and *anointed the feet* of Jesus and washed them with her hair. The beautiful reality depicted here is that when God comes through for you, your worship skyrockets to a higher place and your heart plunges into a greater depth of sacrificial living than you ever imagined possible! Why withhold anything from such a faithful and glorious Savior like Jesus?

Mary of Bethany is seen in the Scriptures as a woman of radical devotion to Jesus Christ. She sat wide-eyed at His feet when all was well, she threw herself at His feet when tragedy struck, and she anointed His feet with costly thanks and praise when her victory broke through! Like Mary, let us determine in all things to be a people *at His feet,* utterly dependent and undistracted in our devotion to Him!

Church of Ephesus

"I know your deeds and your toil and perseverance, and that you cannot tolerate evil men and you put to the test those who call themselves apostles, and they are not, and you found them to be false; and you have perseverance and have endured for My name's sake and have not grown weary. But I have this against you, that you have left your first love. Therefore remember where you have fallen, and repent and do the deeds you did at first"

(Revelation 2:2-5).

The church of Ephesus received these words from Jesus Himself. Without dissecting every piece of this passage, I want to simply point out one thing. These believers were affirmed for all the good they were doing, yet it just wasn't enough. Somewhere along the way they lost sight of being amazed and awed by the beauty and glory of their King. This exhortation resounds throughout the ages to all who are tirelessly laboring in God's harvest but neglecting the secret place of ecstatic delight. God's work doesn't take priority over your relationship with Him. He cares more about the condition of your heart then the work of your hands.

Don't fall victim to idolizing purpose over His presence. Jesus is enough—and He always will be.

"Take it all. Take it all. Just give me Jesus!"

Chapter 5

Divine Hunger

*"How filled you become when you are consumed
with hunger and desire, for you will be completely
satisfied"*

(Luke 6:21 TPT).

Do you hunger for the Lord's presence? Do you long to
know His heart? If so, the abundant life Jesus promised is at
your fingertips. Far too many believers crave everything but
God, and their lifestyles make this unfortunate fact as clear
as day. If that's you, repent and ask God to fill you with
divine hunger. God never intended for hunger to be difficult
to attain; in fact, *it is a gift from God.* Ask Him, and He'll
gladly give it to you. Your desire alone to hunger for God is
proof that you have a measure of hunger that has the power
to connect you to what you want and desperately need.

The Eternal Satisfying Drink

Jesus' parabolic teaching methods would soar over the
heads of the carnally minded and pierce the heart of the
seeking listener. In John 6, He said, "Eat My flesh and drink
My blood" and they immediately assumed He was speaking
about cannibalism. In John 3, Jesus spoke to Nicodemus
about being born again and he responded, "how can a man
enter into his mother's womb and be born a second time?"
Needless to say, he was a bit confused.

In John 4, the Samaritan woman went to Jacob's well to
draw water and Jesus was waiting there for her. Her desire

was to draw natural water to quench the thirst of her physical body. Jesus' desire was to give her a drink of eternal life that would forever eradicate her longing to search elsewhere for pleasure and satisfaction apart from God. "But whoever drinks of the water that I will give him shall never thirst; but the water that I will give him will become in him a well of water springing up to eternal life" (John 4:14).

Some ministers are falsely teaching that hunger is no longer relevant in the new covenant because one taste of Jesus brings eternal satisfaction—according to this passage. The truth that Jesus was highlighting here was that her thirst to search for satisfaction in sinful places would be forever quenched when she tastes of eternal life—not her desire to experience more of God. Hunger is indispensable in the kingdom of God. When God imparts hunger into your innermost being, He's setting you up for an upgrade in the Spirit. If you're content with where you are, that's where you'll stay. You can have as much of God as you'd like. But if your heart aches to see the fullness of God manifest in your life, then you better get ready for a breakthrough of monumental proportions! Divine hunger is a catalyst that takes you from one plateau of glory to another. Jesus loves to satisfy every hungry heart with more of Himself.

An amazing truth about the kingdom of God is that before we were baptized into Christ we were like an arid desert crying out for living water. Then one drink of Jesus caused a well of living water to spring up from within us! You don't need to go here or there to drink from His everlasting stream. He planted His life within you, and you can drink freely whenever and wherever you wish, *by faith*.

Your dry days are over when this truth takes up residence within you.

"Get Hungry!"

I've been to countless meetings where ministers have screamed into a microphone in effort to rouse their congregation, "Get hungry for God! You have to get more hunger for the Lord! Cry out!" The typical outcome is that everyone starts begging God for more hunger and stirring up their emotions to a frenzied state, trying to conjure up spiritual hunger. Then the service ends and everyone goes back to their homes and passes out because they've expended outrageous amounts of emotional energy trying to manufacture this God-given spiritual virtue. The next day they wake up in the same condition they were in before the meeting ever happened. That minister may have looked pious and spiritual for stirring up believers to yell, beg, and cry out for more hunger, but it accomplished little for those who participated. I know God is merciful and I don't doubt the Lord has touched sincere individuals who have taken part in such moments of crying out, but the Lord doesn't bless us just because all our theology and methods are correct. He also doesn't answer our prayers based on how much we plead and beg. If that were the case, then we'd be a people who earn the blessings of God. Blessings can't be earned, they are gifts freely bestowed. He blesses us because He sees past our mess into a pure heart of faith towards Him and He can't help but to bless us.

Let me ask you a question: *Can you crave something that you've never tasted before?* The reason I crave Chick-fil-

A is because I've eaten it and thoroughly enjoyed it. When my stomach starts to growl, chicken tenders, waffle fries and southern sweet tea pops immediately into my mind. Suddenly, my taste buds awaken and my mouth begins to water. Before you know it, I'm in my car, with my eyes on the prize, heading in the direction of the nearest Chick-fil-A. Maybe your guilty pleasures aren't chicken tenders and waffle fries. You may go bonkers over a tasty, juicy cheeseburger at your favorite fast food joint. But the reason you crave cheeseburgers is because you've tasted and seen that they are good. That's how it works.

Compelling people to hunger for God before they've ever had a taste of Him is counterproductive. It's like telling me to hunger for Peking duck, when I have no grid for what it may taste like. As a minister of the gospel, you are called to give people a taste of the Lord. You're a minister of the holy drink—His life-giving presence. You're called to share this good news until people begin to salivate for Him. I won't crave Peking duck until someone explains in detail all the ingredients, the spices used, and the way it's cooked. God's children have been living like paupers, eating the crumbs that fall from the Master's table, yet He's calling you to the wedding feast of the Lamb. Eat freely! Drink up! It's paid for in full. Delight yourself in all that's been given and made readily available in Christ. If you're feeling dry, burnt out, or spiritually malnourished, it's time to run into the arms of Jesus. Let His love, grace, and peace be your delicious feast.

The kingdom of God is upside down from the kingdom of this world in many ways. For instance, in the kingdom of God you aren't discouraged from desiring greatness, but instead of seeking self- exaltation as the road to success, humility and service is the vehicle that takes you there. I heard a pastor profoundly state that in the natural the more you eat physical food, the fuller you become. On the other hand, in the kingdom, the more you eat spiritual food the hungrier you become!

"How filled you become when you are consumed with hunger and desire, for you will be completely satisfied"

(Luke 6:21 TPT).

Cycle of Hunger

An amazing cycle occurs in the spiritual realm. God gives us hunger as a gift, and this hunger compels us to seek Him diligently—resulting in satisfaction and fulfillment. Along with the satisfaction comes more hunger, because it was just too good that you'd be crazy not to want more! Along with your fresh hunger comes and even deeper level of satisfaction and pleasure—and the cycle goes on and on. As Mike Bickle accurately explains:

"The Creator places longings within us which can only be answered by and in Him. He then answers the longings in part, giving us just enough satisfaction to sustain us in the pursuit, and leaving just enough of an ache to keep us on the journey. The nature of being wooed demands an ebb and flow of desire and satisfaction."[1]

Hunger is our escort into deep and lasting spiritual satisfaction. Suddenly, you begin to realize that you're living far below your inheritance in Christ, and a blessing in disguise called *"divine dissatisfaction"* begins to set in. A spiritual stirring follows as you begin to hunger for more of God. This is a supernatural orchestration from God to woo your heart into the "deep cries out to deep" relationship He longs to have with you. *On the other side of your hunger is an encounter with His glory.*

A friend of mine once told me, "I'm so hungry for God, but I feel like I'm never being filled up as the Scriptures promise." At that time, my friend didn't understand the work of the Holy Spirit within him. It's impossible for you to hunger for God without the Holy Spirit present, imparting to you the hunger you're feeling. In fact, it's the Spirit's influence on your new-creation heart that breeds hunger for the Lord in the first place. Therefore, if you feel hungry for God, it's proof that He is near and present supplying the hunger. In turn, you can rest in His nearness and enjoy intimacy with Him in your hunger. After all, Jesus is the hungry One, He is the thirsty One—and He thirsts for your undivided attention and affection. Before He breathed His last on the cross He uttered the words, *"I thirst."* He hungers and thirsts for you more than you ever could for Him. If you hunger for God, then it's God *in you* producing that hunger. In that moment of hungering for more, choose to set your mind on the reality that it's Him inside of you playing your heartstrings to the tune of His love and passionate pursuit. He's drawing you into the song of all songs: the song of divine romance with Him.

Let me make this point a bit clearer: Let's say the Holy Spirit decides one day that He's had enough of humanity and completely withdraws Himself from the earth altogether.

First of all, the earth would spontaneously combust because God even holds the world on its axis by the word of His power, but that's beside the point. Let's say all is well, but the Holy Spirit decides "no more!" and retreats to heaven to hang out with the Father and the Son. Humanity would immediately morph into the most toxic, demonic God-haters who have ever graced the face of this planet. Why? Because without God's glory we're absolutely hopeless and depraved in every sense of the word. If the glory of God departed entirely, then no hunger, longing, or acknowledgment of God would be found in the land of the living. God is the very Light of mankind. "In Him was life, and the life was the Light of men" (John 1:4). *His glory is our glory.*

Even unbelievers who walk in love, mercy, and kindness are exuding the very nature and essence of God. Yes, unbelievers aren't born again and haven't been washed of their sins—but they still are image-bearers of our Triune God. They've been created in His image and likeness like the rest of us. The image is just tainted and, in some cases, marred beyond recognition.

The deceiver has duped the church into believing the lie of lack and distance. "For out of His fullness [the superabundance of His grace and truth] we have all received grace upon grace [spiritual blessing upon spiritual blessing, favor upon favor, and gift heaped upon gift]" (John 1:16 AMP). You lack nothing, child of God, and it is vital that *you believe that.* Faith and hunger go hand in hand in the kingdom. You must believe that you have everything you need in Christ, while simultaneously refusing to tolerate less than God's best for you! Hunger divorced from faith becomes mere emotionalism, void of power to effect change. The type of hunger that Jesus spoke about in the Beatitudes is possessed with faith! Therefore, hunger and faith partner together to release the manifestation.

The only way to produce more hunger is to keep feasting on Him. All is provided friends. Eat freely and drink of His presence—drink until your heart's content. *Then drink some more!*

Seeking Him

I've heard some preachers teach that seeking God is an Old Testament concept, no longer relevant to new-covenant believers. Ultimately, Jesus *is* the seeker in the relationship, but that truth by no means invalidates the participation and cooperation that's vital in our relationship with Him.

These ministers fight to emphasize the truth of Jesus being the Husband who pursues His bride, but at the same time they diminish an integral truth found in God's Word. We know that no one can come to God unless the Father draws them first; therefore all our seeking is only a result of His empowering grace. Yet the apostle James challenges believers to draw near to God so that God will draw near to them. Just because you're currently receiving revelation of God's wild and fervent pursuit of you, doesn't mean you throw away all the other passages that plainly speak of your pursuit of Him. What about Hebrews 11:6 that says God rewards those who diligently seek Him? That's written to believers under the new covenant. What about Jesus' teaching about asking, seeking, and knocking? Just because Jesus taught under the old covenant system doesn't mean that everything He taught was the Law. In His infinite mind, He knew that these words would be scribed for generations to come to live by.

Though this is true, the reality that I believe needs stronger emphasis in the church today is that we aren't seeking a distant God, far off, aloof in the clouds somewhere and grossly impossible to reach. The God we seek is *Christ in us*. He's closer than the air that you breathe. He's within you. You can't get any closer than inside of you! How intimate is that? Seek Him—you won't have to look too far. He's right there. All around you, filling the atmosphere as you set your heart and mind on Him. He's in the innermost part of your being.

Seeking His Hands

I served in Mozambique as a missionary with Iris Global, and the work they are doing is absolutely remarkable. I strongly recommend you look up Iris and check out the amazing miracles and acts of mercy taking place around the world as an extension of this ministry. The lives of so many people are being turned right-side up for God's kingdom.

While in Mozambique we lived among the poor, orphaned, and afflicted. The Lord gave me a stronger dose of compassion for a few young boys who lived there. Supernaturally, divine love gripped me for these boys. The only problem was that they were masterminds at ripping off westerners. They were professionals at coercing you to buy them food, clothes, electronics, and all kinds of things. Because I am white, they assumed I was swimming in cash. When it boiled down to it—though I was living by faith—I still had more than them. Frequently, God would lead me to take them out for lunch and show them His unconditional love. Every time I saw them, it wasn't "Hello Michael, how are you today? We missed you and want to play!" It was more like, "Give me chicken. I want a soda. Give me money."

My heart would break because all I wanted was to spend time with them, and in their eyes I was only a big, white dollar sign. One afternoon, the boys approached me with joy on their faces. One boy grabbed my hand and the other hugged my side. I melted as I imagined our interaction to go differently because of their loving approach. After about ten seconds of affection, they began to ask me with their well-practiced begging voices, "Michael, will you buy me chicken? Soda? Give me money, please?" Immediately, I became saddened by their incessant asking and begging. Holy Spirit then said to me, "Son, this is how I feel when My people draw near to Me only to get the blessings that flow from My hands, and not to seek My face for who I am."

When these children came only seeking material things, I was experiencing the same hurt and pain that God feels when His bride seeks Him predominantly for material things. How would any husband feel if his wife only loved on him when she wanted to make a large purchase? I bet it wouldn't feel good at all. God does desire to bless His children, but we must get our priorities straight. Our hearts must always yearn for Him above all else. *His presence must be our priority.*

Check your prayer life and see if most of your prayers consist of asking God for *things*. If you're constantly making petitions, seeking promotions, praying for a spouse, more souls, a bigger house, a brand new car, etc., than your prayer life needs a serious makeover. It's okay to ask Him for things, but you'll only receive that which is according to His will. The more you seek His face over His hands the more your heart and God's heart will become intrinsically synchronized and united as one entity. Your spirit is already one with God, now your mind, will and emotions are learning to align with that spiritual reality.

Before you know it, His will and desires will be melded into one with your will and desires. You'll begin to hunger for whatever is God's best for you. Prayer is meant to be personal. Thank Him for all His blessings. Sing songs of love and praise because of who He is. Dig into the Word of God and discover what it says about who you are and how He sees you. Speak in tongues and release His perfect will over your circumstances. Worship Him because He's worthy of all your affection! Quiet your soul and meditate on His forever-enduring mercies.

In the beginning of everyone's walk with the Lord, crying out to God for help, refuge, and blessings is quite common. But after you eat of Him, taste of His kindness towards you, and experience the riches of His wrap-around glory, your prayer life radically shifts. Instead of always praying for "things" your heart cry becomes, "all I want is more of You, Lord." You recognize that His nearness is more important than anything else this world has to offer. Simply put, *nothing beats Jesus*.

What Are You Feeding On?

The reason so many believers can't maintain spiritual hunger is because they are feeding themselves on so many other things. Whatever you feed on, you will hunger for.

If you're constantly playing video games, that's what you'll crave. If you're spending hours of your day scrolling through social media, every time boredom strikes or a split second of awkwardness arises in a social setting, you'll run to your phone for refuge. In addition, if your mind is always thinking of sports, stats, fantasy football, and the like, you'll constantly gravitate toward that like its second nature. Listen: there is nothing wrong with playing video games (depending on the game), and there is nothing evil about spending time on your smart phone (depending on what you're looking at), and God isn't against sports, but do you find yourself consumed with everything else besides Jesus? Are you finding time to think about Him, get into His Word, and worship Him in the splendor of holiness? Does the Lord cross your mind throughout the day, or only on Sunday mornings at church? There's something wrong, saints of God, if you know the stats of every sports player you admire but can't quote chapter and verse of your favorite Bible Scripture.

The more you feed on God's Word and spend time in His presence, the more you will long for time with Him. When you do, discipline mystically transforms into a delight beyond comprehension. There have been times when the Lord told me to put down my phone and turn off social media because it was preoccupying all my time and attention. Don't misunderstand me, I enjoy my smart phone, and social media is fine, but instead of wasting precious time scrolling down your screen for hours, you could be getting your *face* into His *book*, caught up in intimacy with the Holy Spirit.

There was a time when I was picking up odd jobs for a limo company to make a few extra dollars when I first got married to my wife, Selina. One night, I was waiting for the plane to land and passing time on social media. Out of nowhere, I heard the Holy Spirit speak to me, *"You're distracted and preoccupied with your phone when you could be spending time with Me."* Immediately, I put my phone down and started to pray. After a few minutes my mind drifted off again and out of habit I unconsciously picked up my phone. Realizing that my mind had wandered, I put my phone down again and I resumed praying. I started by simply thanking Him, praising Him, and speaking in tongues out loud. Suddenly, the Spirit took over and it wasn't me praying anymore, but Christ praying through me. I was taken into a vision and I saw the Father sitting on His throne. He called me to Himself and I ran into His arms. Laughter filled His throne room as He held me tightly and hugged me again and again. I melted in His eternal embrace. My heavenly Father affirmed me with His love and uplifted me with His mighty presence. *All was well with my soul.*

Then Cambodia popped into my head. Thought after thought ran through my mind as I remembered words spoken and the wonderful time I had there ministering the year before. Suddenly, I knew that God was calling Selina and I to go to Cambodia and serve alongside a close friend's ministry there for that upcoming season. All I could think about after that encounter was *What if I didn't respond to His invitation to come close? What if I shrugged it off and kept flipping through my phone occupying my time? How many words and revelations have I forfeited because of*

distraction and absorption with the temporal luxuries of life?
It doesn't have to be evil for it to be an idol; it just needs to
serve as a distraction that pulls you away from investing in
your relationship with God.

A True Fast

A close friend of mine told me that he was fasting food
once a week for three months in effort to get more "spiritual."
If you were wondering, by the way, that is the wrong type of
fasting. My friend told me that he didn't receive anything that
he could remember from those times of separated fasting and
prayer. However, the Lord did make one thing clear to him—
he'd been spending too much time on the computer,
watching movies, and playing video games.

He responded by pulling away from those things for a
season and focused on spending time with the Lord instead.
As a result, he found himself revolutionized by the truths,
revelations, and personal breakthroughs he received in that
time. He was dumbfounded by what he received through
investing time and energy in his relationship with the Lord,
instead of the innocent, yet time-consuming activities that
previously distracted him. When he was telling me his
story, Hosea 6:6 (NIV) came to mind, "For I desire mercy,
not sacrifice, and acknowledgment of God rather than
burnt offerings."

The Lord doesn't desire sacrifice—*He desires
acknowledgement of Him.* Fasting isn't about abstaining
from food or any other natural pleasure. Fasting is
primarily about recalibration. Many believers think they are
gaining "brownie points" in heaven by fasting on a regular

basis. It's not your sacrifice that moves God; it's your drawing near to Him. Throughout the Old Testament, God blessed the people with tenacity enough to simply acknowledge and believe in Him amid a perverse and unbelieving generation.

Fasting is good and holy when done right, and is meant to be about setting aside time to indulge in a blissful feast of union with Jesus Christ. For a time, give up whatever is stealing your devotion to Him who is worthy of it all. Feed your soul on God's presence and Word and you'll begin to hunger for Him day and night.

God Over Food!

On numerous occasions I have had powerful encounters with the Lord during unplanned fasts. Here's one story of many that may help explain my point. A woman who is known for being a prophetess came into town once to minister at a conference in Dallas, Texas. The service started at six, and I was already running late but I hadn't eaten dinner yet. Suddenly, I had a choice to make. I could eat dinner, arrive late and miss a large portion of the worship. Or I could skip dinner, go straight to the meeting, and experience every bit of what God was doing in that place. An internal war was waged, but my spiritual hunger prevailed and I darted to the service instead.

After worship, the minister immediately began to prophesy. She said, "If you're called to live in remote parts of the world as a missionary, I want you to come up here now!" About a third of the auditorium stormed the altar, myself included.

This minister never called me out personally, but she didn't need to—because God targeted me Himself. Suddenly, I began to feel electricity in my hands and feet. My body started to shake, yet I stopped myself because I didn't want to be seen as *weird* to the people around me. Eventually, I threw caution to the wind and opened my heart to God, asking Him to have His way. *Wham!* The electricity of His Spirit shot through my entire body and I fell backwards to the floor—*and stayed there.* On that floor, God revealed to me some of the most life-altering truths about my identity and call that have remained with me to this day. It wasn't my abstaining from natural food that pleased God—it was my spiritual hunger to choose Him above all else. I wanted Jesus, more then I wanted dinner— *and He honored my hunger with divine encounter.*

I once heard a preacher say, "Many Christians are chasing an encounter with God! I don't want an encounter of a lifetime—I want a lifetime of encounters!" Well, I'd have to say that both sound good to me. I'll take a lifetime of encounters with an encounter of a lifetime on the side, please.

Jesus is stirring a holy appetite in His people for divine realities. He's opening our eyes to see into the realm of the Spirit. Instead of storing up earthly treasures and focusing all our energy on building a natural kingdom, let's place highest value on storing up heavenly treasures that will never rust or perish. After all, when we see Him face-to-face in eternity, all of our earthly pursuits apart from Him will turn to ash and amount to nothing.

My prayer is that this book would impart holy hunger into your innermost being. I pray that you'd set yourself up for an encounter with Jesus Christ. Never neglect the secret place and continue to cultivate a lifestyle of seeking, knocking and asking with the Lord—because He's promised to be found, answer, and give you all you're asking for.

> "It would not be an exaggeration to call this hunger a 'burning within.' It is ignited by God, but sustained through the cooperation of the individual."
>
> —Bill Johnson[2]

Chapter 6

Faith's Access

"In whom [Jesus] *we have boldness and confident access through faith in Him"*

(Ephesians 3:12).

Sadly, many churches have reduced salvation to "repeat this prayer after me." Then, when the prayer is over the minister asks for those who have prayed this "salvation prayer" for the first time to raise their hands so they can be acknowledged for receiving Jesus as their Lord and Savior. My heart is burdened over how many people I've seen pray this prayer, and then leave church in the same condition that they came. I believe it's because we don't explain the true biblical meaning of faith and the necessity of laying down one's life. Instead of caring more about the salvation of the lost, many pastors and ministers care more about how many hands raise after the prayer to validate their ministry. Preachers have misused Romans 10:9 where the apostle Paul writes, "If you declare with your mouth, 'Jesus is Lord,' and believe in your heart that God raised him from the dead, you will be saved" (Romans 10:9 NIV).

How can someone be born again, and yet show no evidence of true internal transformation by the Spirit of God? Have we diminished the power of the new birth? Aren't we supposed to be transformed into brand new creations? If you have truly received the grace of God, you'll begin to show evidence of internal change. That doesn't mean you'll never sin again—it just means you'll begin to develop a strong distaste for sin as you drink deeply of God's unfathomable grace.

Salvation cannot be placed in a neatly-packaged prayer box. Repeating a prayer after a pastor isn't your ticket to heaven, but placing your life into the hands of Jesus is. Don't get me wrong, many have been saved praying in this manner, but it wasn't the "prayer" that saved them—it was their sincerity of faith behind the prayer. I've heard it said that many roads lead to Jesus, but there is only *one road* that leads to the Father. Meaning, it doesn't matter how you get to Jesus, as long as you get to Him. It could be through an answered altar call or a divine encounter—there is no formula. The heart of faith is what counts.

Saying you believe in Jesus simply isn't enough. A lot of you may disagree with that statement thinking that it's too harsh and even unbiblical. But the Bible tells us that even the demons believe in Him and shudder (James 2:19). Growing up in church or having a praying grandmother isn't the right criteria to gain eternal life. From God's perspective, the biblical kind of faith is the only kind there is. Faith doesn't originate in the human mind within our logic or reasoning, but true faith springs up from the deepest part of our hearts. It's the only natural response to seeing the outrageous and lavished gift of God's grace towards us. The gospel is impossible to understand intellectually. Your heart and spirit must lead the way, and your brain catches up later. In this chapter, I will venture into the vast subject of faith and how it pertains to abiding in the presence of God.

True Faith

Faith is the essence of the Christian life. Jesus said, "When the Son of Man comes, will He find faith on the earth?" (Luke 18:8). As I hear those words I don't hear one trace of condemnation or anger. I hear the broken heart of Christ expressing His deep longing for a people who would abandon themselves in wholehearted trust in Him.

There's no denying that faith is a constant theme throughout the Scriptures. The Bible says that it's impossible to please God without faith (Hebrews 11:6). The righteous man shall live by faith (Romans 1:17). Believers are to walk by faith, not by sight (2 Corinthians 5:7). The only way to be saved is by grace *through faith* (Ephesians 2:8). All people are justified and have peace with God through faith (Romans 5:1). And the Scripture I really want to unpack here is Ephesians 3:12, which says, "In [Jesus] we have boldness and confident access *through faith in Him.*" Paul boldly declares that you can be confident that you have access into God's presence through faith in Jesus Christ. That's truly amazing! Before we dive into this truth a bit deeper, let's explore the true nature of faith.

The way the world uses the word *believe* is completely different from the biblical meaning. To many, believing has more to do with agreeing intellectually with a set of facts than the Bible's definition of true believing. Belief and faith are used interchangeably throughout the Scriptures. I believe the Amplified Bible says it best. Take a look at this Scripture below:

"We have had the glad tidings [Gospel of God] proclaimed to us just as truly as they...but the

*message they heard did not benefit them, because it was not mixed with **faith (with the leaning of the entire personality on God in absolute trust and confidence in His power, wisdom, and goodness)** by those who heard it; neither were they united in faith with the ones [Joshua and Caleb] who heard (did believe). For we who have **believed (adhered to and trusted in and relied on God)** do enter that rest"*

(Hebrews 4:2-3 AMP).

According to the above text, faith is defined as follows:

1. Leaning your entire personality on God in absolute trust and confidence in His power, wisdom, and goodness.

2. To adhere to, trust in, and rely on God.

I like to refer to faith as confident trust—full assurance. Faith believes God's Word over contrary feelings and circumstances. It doesn't matter what someone else says to you; if you've heard from God, and it's a promise in His Word—it's final. If your world is falling apart around you—you know God will pull you through. Genuine faith produces peace in your soul even when a storm is raging all around you. The life of faith is what establishes you in the rest of God (more on this subject in a later chapter). Life's process in Christ is learning to live by faith, not by your natural sight or the sporadic feelings that rage violently within you.

I bet you know a lot of people who say they are "believers" in Jesus, but how many of these people lean upon Him with their whole being in absolute trust in His power, wisdom, and goodness? How many of those people trust in, rely upon, and adhere to Christ in every circumstance of their lives? *How about you?*

Our faith plugs us into the power of God that is latent in His Word. Your circumstances don't dictate your faith, *your faith dictates your circumstances.* Faith isn't moved by the natural order of things—faith moves the natural order of things. As believers the only battle that remains is the fight of faith. And the good news is that we aren't fighting *for* victory, we're fighting *from* victory. Jesus already won and we now get to enforce His victory through kingdom works infused with faith! Now let's see how faith becomes our access into the glory of our union with Jesus.

Our Sacred Access

Faith is the key by which we unlock the treasury of the fullness of God. The riches of our spiritual inheritance begin to materialize as we learn to trust Him, stand on His promises and act on them.

> *"Everything heaven contains has already been lavished upon us as a love gift from our wonderful heavenly Father, the Father of our Lord Jesus—all because he sees us wrapped into Christ. This is why we celebrate him with all our hearts!"*
>
> (Ephesians 1:3 TPT).

Because this is reality, and all of heaven's blessings are fully ours in Christ, then faith is surely your access that brings about a manifestation of these blessings into your life. Faith is the pin code that enables you to withdraw from your heavenly bank account. Jesus benevolently graced you with every spiritual blessing, and you access these spiritual riches by trusting in His unchanging nature and promises. *Believing is receiving in the kingdom of God.*

Brother Lawrence stated, "The trust we put in God honors Him so much, and draws down great graces."[1] I've also heard it said that faith is like Wi-Fi—it's invisible, but it has the power to connect you to all that you need. Because faith brings such delight to God's heart, He has made it our connector to the divine—the unseen spiritual realm. On the other hand, it was faithlessness that brought about the catastrophe of the fall of man in the Garden of Eden. Adam and Eve shifted their trust from God and His words to satan and his words—and the rest is history. Many believe that the fall of man was the result of disobedience. In one sense, this is true. But all sin originates from one place—*an unbelieving heart*. We can see now that faith is of utmost importance in our Christian lives.

Faith Before the Manifestation

I use to believe that if I prayed enough, fasted enough, or separated myself unto Him in greater ways, then He'd give me more of His presence. This was an absolute lie.

A staple Scripture is Galatians 3:12, which tells us that "The law is not of faith." Paul wrote this to the believers in Galatia when they strayed from the simplicity of the gospel, being deceived by a group of people called the Judaizers. The great apostle preached salvation by grace through faith alone. Yet these Judaizers preached that faith wasn't enough and that obedience to the Law of Moses—adherence to fleshly circumcision and the necessity of honoring certain Jewish holy days—were essential to being saved. Needless to say, Paul wasn't too happy about this.

What Paul learned in his years of zeal and unfettered passion is that you can't earn the love, grace, and presence of God. All is grace. All is a gift. Obeying the Law and engaging in spiritual practices can't earn you entrance into the blessings of His presence. Our access into the fullness of His glory *is faith alone.* How do you go deeper in God? *Faith* is your divine connector, not any dead works to climb the spiritual ladder yourself.

You gain access into the Spirit by believing *that you are already in the Spirit.* You access the presence of God by believing *you are already in His presence.* In fact, you are seated with Christ in the heavenly places (Ephesians 2:6). You have been seated in His presence for all eternity. *Your home is His throne room.* Smith Wigglesworth, a great man of faith, said this:

> "Beloved, I see all the plan of life where God comes in and vindicates His power and makes His presence felt. It is not by crying or groaning. It is because we believe. And yet, I have nothing to say about it except that sometimes it takes God a long time to bring us through groaning and crying before we can believe."[2]

You may ask, "If my works don't grant me access into God's presence, how come I've had radical encounters when I've fasted, prayed and read the Bible extensively?" Fantastic question, and the answer is simple. Each of these practices don't earn you anything from God, but they do turn your heart's attention to Jesus Christ, the Author and Finisher of your faith. As you turn to Him, faith begins to grow within you, which brings about a manifestation of your breakthrough. Let me say it a slightly different way. Sometimes the motivation of our devotion to the Lord unconsciously stems from a "works mentality." Instead of seeking His face from a sincere place of faith and love, we strive to twist God's arms to do what we want Him to do. Thank God, at some point along the way we glimpse His glory and raw faith rises up within us! Consequently, we receive exactly what we need because all answers are found in His presence. The problem is never on God's side of the equation; it's always on ours. Like Smith Wigglesworth stated above, "sometimes it takes God a long time to bring us through groaning and crying before we can believe."

You aren't meant to live by your feelings—your feelings can lie to you. If you don't feel God's presence, that doesn't negate that fact that He's within you and all around you. Just because you aren't hearing God speak, doesn't mean He's not speaking. Just because you feel powerless, doesn't mean you truly are. Trusting in the Word of God, over your feelings, people's opinions, or your adverse circumstances is your key to experiencing the "more of God" that's available to you.

Feelings don't precede faith; faith precedes feelings. What I mean by that is—you can't trust what your feelings tell you on a regular basis. But if you learn to trust in God's Word in each situation in your life, you'll find that faith will produce in you godly emotions that will be a wellspring of delight and enjoyment. Peace, joy, and love will flood your innermost being. His tangible, powerful presence will overtake you! The power of God will touch people as you pray for them. You don't need to feel fire in your hands, tingles, or goosebumps to know God is working on someone you're praying for. It's nice when you do have those feelings, but it won't always happen that way. Trust that Jesus commanded us to lay hands on the sick and He promised results! *Faith comes before feelings, and faith comes before the manifestation.*

A devastating corruption that entered into humanity through the fall is that humans have learned to think and live carnally instead of spiritually. The apostle Paul calls believers several times in his epistles "fleshly" or "worldly." They live by their five senses over the truth of God's Word. Let's grow in His Spirit and be a people of His Word.

The Torn Veil

In this section, I want to shed light on an area of truth that will set you free if you allow it to sink into your heart. Listen to what I'm about to say with the ears of your spirit, not your natural mind. *Sin never separated God from you, but it did separate you from God.* Read that statement again, but slower this time. Sin doesn't turn God's heart away from you; instead it hardens your hearts towards Him. In fact, He pursues the lost sheep and seeks diligently for the lost coin. He is drawn to our areas of darkness and weakness so He can be our Redeemer, Helper, and Comforter. God hates sin, not because His holiness is offended, but because His holy love can't stand to see sin wreak havoc on His loved ones.

> *"Encourage one another daily, as long as it is called 'Today,' so that none of you may be hardened by sin's deceitfulness"*
>
> (Hebrews 3:13 NIV).

Sin has detrimental effects on the human heart: shame, guilt, condemnation, fear, pain, trauma, and more. Sin brought sickness, poverty, and death into the world. Sin will destroy your life and cause you to wound the people around you.

Believing that sin separates you from God will rob you from the depth of intimacy that is available in Christ. Believing one minute you're in the light and the next minute you're in the darkness—going back and forth based on your obedience—is a lie that steals from your union with Christ. The truth is that you have been rescued from the domain of darkness and transferred into the kingdom of God's beloved Son (Colossians 1:13). You aren't going back and forth based on your performance. In the same way, the Holy Spirit doesn't leave you when you sin, and come back into your body when you repent. He's always there. He's always drawing you to repentance. You wouldn't have any desire to repent if the Holy Spirit wasn't living in you, imparting the very desire. If God turned His face from you when you sinned, you'd be absolutely hopeless. *Your repentance doesn't turn God's heart back to you; it turns your heart back to Him.* God's not the one that needs changing—we do. Jesus didn't come to change God's mind about you, He came to change your mind about God. Our heavenly Father's mind didn't need changing, "For God so loved the world, that He gave His only begotten Son" (John 3:16).

Let's look at Adam and Eve for a moment. If God were to be mad at anyone it would be them. They got us in this mess in the first place! Yet, how did God respond when they disobeyed His command? *He pursued them.* It was Adam and Eve who covered their nakedness because of shame, hiding in the bushes from their loving Creator and Father. God is the One who sought them asking, "Where are you guys?" The Lord was the initiator in the conversation. He didn't withdraw or withhold Himself—*He drew near.* In His mercy and love, He killed the first animal, took the skin, and covered their nakedness as a prophetic picture of Jesus, our sacrificial Lamb. The Bible reveals God to be the one who offers the sacrifices that count. He offered the first sacrifice in the Garden of Eden to cover Adam and Eve's sin. Again, He provided a ram in the thicket in place of Abraham's son, revealing Himself as the One who supplies the perfect sacrifice. Finally, through His Son, Jesus, He nullified the need for any further sacrifices to ever be made. It was the sacrifice of all sacrifices!

Likewise, in the story of Cain and Abel, God is the One who approached Cain after he killed his brother. The Lord strolled up and asked Cain, "Where is your brother?" Cain then responded arrogantly with an unrepentant heart, "Am I my brother's keeper?" Cain sinned, and reaped the consequences of his actions, but again, it's plain to see that God is the One who approached him, even in his sinfulness. He didn't wait for Cain to be sorrowful and repent. Our heavenly Father is the Seeker in this relationship. He's the Pursuer of the lost sheep. He's the Initiator in the heart of every sinner. Sin doesn't separate God from you or cause Him to turn His face away from you in disgust!

You may be thinking: *Yes, but when the sin of the world fell on Jesus didn't the Father forsake Him and look away?* Many of us grew up believing that because of Jesus' words on the cross, "My God, My God, why have You forsaken Me?"

At surface level it seems like the only logical interpretation, yet it runs far deeper than that. In 2 Corinthians 5:19, Paul said that "God was in Christ reconciling the world to Himself." That means God was *in* Christ, unseen to the natural eye, working the reconciliation of all things. The night before Jesus was betrayed to be crucified, He said to His disciples, "A time is coming and in fact has come when you will be scattered, each to your own home. You will leave me all alone. Yet I am not alone, for my Father is with me" (John 16:32 NIV). God didn't leave Jesus for one moment. God has never and will never forsake anyone. It's not in His nature.

You may respond, "But isn't God too holy to look upon sin?" If that were the case, then the whole world would be hopeless because it's steeped in sin! God doesn't close His eyes when you sin because He's too holy to look at you sinning. He sees your sin, sympathizes with you, weeps with you, and offers you a hand to lift you up from the ground. When our sin fell upon Jesus at the cross, He experienced the full ramifications of our sin, including the psychological torment that comes along with it. Sin deceives us into believing that we are forsaken by God and He is angry with us. Adam and Eve hid from God because of their sin, and God chased after them. Sin makes us feel forsaken by God, but forsaking us never even crossed His mind. On the cross, Jesus felt what we feel when we sin. He saw through our broken lenses. Our cry became His cry on the cross. "My God, why have You forsaken Me?" He felt forsaken by God, like we often do, in order for you and me to never feel forsaken again—but fully accepted in the beloved Son. Because Jesus was not only fully God, but fully man, He had to experience our depravity in the fullest sense. This statement of anguish perfectly reveals the depth of all He went through on our behalf. He truly is the great High Priest who sympathizes entirely with all of our weaknesses, because He was tempted in every way that we are.

The veil of sin in your heart that separated you from God was torn in two through your faith in what Christ has done for you. Sin's power is broken and you've been eternally forgiven because of your eternal redemption. God has made you holy through the blood of His Son and you're suitable to enter into His glorious presence—*sin or no sin*. Sin doesn't separate you from God. Period. You can approach Him whenever you wish for all the comfort, peace, hope, joy, power, and freedom that you need. God used to live in the temple in Jerusalem, and a thick dark veil separated man from God's manifest glory. When Christ died on the cross, the veil was torn in two from *top to bottom—not bottom to top.* Why is that significant? Because humanity (bottom) couldn't climb back into God's presence on its own—Jesus (top) needed to step down and carry us back into the glory of God. In His holy passion, God Himself tore the veil, never to be seen again.

Beloved, the veil of sin has been removed—yet unbelief can act as a veil that separates us from experiencing the fullness of our God-given inheritance. Trusting in your own obedience to God as the proper means to entering His presence will get you nowhere fast. Instead, trust that you freely have unhindered access to the heart of Daddy God, His glorious presence, and His magnificent promises—through faith in Jesus Christ.

Faith Comes by Hearing

You may be wondering, if this is true, "How do I grow my faith?"

"So faith comes from hearing, and hearing by the word of Christ"

(Romans 10:17).

This Scripture has become foundational for me. Making the Word of God your daily feast will cause great faith to spring up from deep within you. Whatever situation you're in, find a promise Scripture that you can stand on in the midst of it all.

For example, if financial burdens are weighing you down, start speaking over yourself, "The Lord is my shepherd, I lack nothing" (Psalm 23:1 NIV). Hearing the Word of God will eventually cause great faith to be the driving force of your life in the area you apply it. If you sow apple seeds, you'll reap a harvest of apples. It will take time, but eventually the harvest will come. The same goes with God's Word. If you sow His Word into the soil of your heart, you will reap the kind of promise that you've planted and watered. Be patient, it's a process.

Before I do anything in the morning I offer to the Lord the first fruit of my lips. I declare His Word, "I am dearly loved and accepted by God. I am His beloved son in whom He's well pleased. I am as righteous as He is righteous. I am His joy and His delight. Jesus is in me and I am in Him." As I speak the Word of God, I'm hearing His words come from my lips, and faith comes by hearing! Consequently, faith is rising up within me and it lifts me up into an ecstatic experience of intimacy in His presence.

Try not to speak negatively about your situation—determine to only speak faith-filled words. If someone asks you, "How's the money coming in for your upcoming mission trip?" and it currently isn't looking so hot, choose to speak faith-filled words like, "I'm still believing, but He's faithful to provide all my needs." I love to quote Hudson Taylor, "I have 25 cents and all the promises of God."[3]

Hearers Only

In hearing God's Word, it's crucial to set our hearts upon receiving those words by faith. Check out what the apostle James had to say about this:

> *"Don't just listen to the Word of Truth and not respond to it, for that is the essence of self-deception. So always let His word become like poetry written and fulfilled by your life. If you listen to the Word and don't live out the message you hear, you become like the person who looks in the mirror of the Word to discover the reflection of his face in the beginning. You perceive how God sees you in the mirror of the Word but then you go out and forget your divine origin"*
>
> (James 1:22-24 TPT).

This Scripture informs us that it's possible to hear God's Word without it having a substantial impact on our hearts. How is this possible when, according to Romans 10:17, faith comes by hearing and hearing the Word of Christ? I'm sure you know of someone that has many Scriptures memorized, but it hasn't made an impact on his or her way of life. They are hearing God's Word, even memorizing it, but it hasn't been translated from their head to their heart.

As humans with a free will, you can either harden your heart to God's Word, or you can yield your heart to His Word. Applying faith to God's promises activates the ever-present power hidden within (which was there all along). The Word of God is powerful, whether you believe it or not. But you won't see its effects until you give it the place of importance it deserves. For instance, you can sing a song out of habit without your heart being engaged with the lyrics. This happens to me all the time. I'll be singing a worship song yet my mind is pondering my daily responsibilities. When I notice this happening I begin to refocus and engage my heart with the lyrics of adoration. As a result, the river begins to flow and the Holy Spirit carries me into an intimate time of worship with my King!

In today's social media age, we have access to the most anointed revelation and teachings. All you have to do is go on the Internet to listen to a message from just about any minister you wish. You can login to any of the numerous social media outlets and hear the word of the day from the most credible and dynamic teachers out there. The temptation is to read their statuses and say "amen," click Like, and continue to scroll down the page without ever giving it a second thought. What ever happened to taking the Word of God and hiding it in our hearts?

You can't attend church on Sunday, hear the pastor share an inspiring, anointed biblical message, never think about it again, and pray it changes your life. It doesn't work that way. You must receive the words of Christ into your heart. The gospel must be valued and honored by taking up a place of preeminence in your life. You must begin to filter everything you do through the reality of God's Word.

Theology just won't do it. Ritualistic church services can't give you what you need most. His words must transcend past theological truths into "Word made flesh" in our lives. He wants to possess you with His Word so much so that you become a living, breathing exhibition of His glory everywhere that you go.

True faith isn't mental assent. Faith originates in the heart, not the head. Faith is total trust and reliance on God and His unchanging Word. If you want to grow in your relationship with Jesus, growing in faith is key. Faith is your access into the richness of God's presence and the magnificent spiritual blessings that are yours in Christ.

> "Faith really consists of knowing who God is. It consists of becoming familiar with His glory and majesty—because those who know Him best trust Him the most."
>
> —David Wilkerson[4]

Chapter 7

Embrace Grace

"The Word became flesh and made his dwelling among us. We have seen his glory, the glory of the one and only Son, who came from the Father, full of grace and truth"

(John 1:14 NIV).

It's impossible to go deeper in Christ without gaining a revelation of the grace of God. Jesus is *full of grace and truth.* As you look upon Him, *you look upon grace personified.* Developing a lifestyle of looking unto Jesus and fixing your eyes on Him is the lifestyle of living by grace. You'll find that His grace will infuse every area you include Him in.

The grace of Christ is the offense of the gospel. Every believer must face this reality head on. Condemnation, guilt, and shame conquer the hearts of countless true lovers of God. If you don't allow the Holy Spirit to deal with these prevalent and sensitive issues of your heart through the wonderworking power of His grace, you'll begin to stagnate in your spiritual growth. My intention in this chapter is for you to become possessed by a revelation of God's grace so you can step boldly into God's presence in every situation in life.

Parable of the Wall

Let me share with you a parable to help illustrate my point. A strong wall stands tall a few miles down on the road to life, blocking the path for the king's royal servants to continue their journey. None of the king's servants know how to conquer this wall, so each of them decides to face it differently.

The first servant sees the wall and is intimidated. After failing to come up with a plan, he decides to pitch a tent and stay there. Day after day, he hopes that he'll eventually muster up enough motivation and strategy to get across, but sadly, he stays stagnant and never advances on his journey.

A second servant is absolutely desperate to make it to the other side. His heart is right, but his strategy is way off. He thinks that if he keeps hitting the wall over and over again with all his might, one day it will surely disintegrate or topple over. Frustrated, all he has to show for himself are bruises and broken knuckles. In the end, he gives up.

The last servant arrives. He devises an elaborate plan to make a rope, toss it over the top, and climb safely to the other side. After many failed attempts, he takes a moment and comes to an astute, game-changing conclusion. He can't do it on his own. The kind, gracious, compassionate king comes to his mind. He had promised to help him with any obstacle that arose. The servant sends word, and the king comes to his aid and helps him over the impossible wall.

In this parable, the wall represents the personal obstacles that hinder our spiritual progress. For some, it's self-condemnation; for others, it's a refusal to step out of comfort zones, while others are heavily restricted by fears. Regardless of what it is for you, we all face giants in our walk with the Lord. How do we react when these giants confront us? Do we allow them to hinder us?

The first man who pitched a tent represents those who have good intentions yet are comfortable with where they are on the journey. They are okay with attending church, hanging out with "Christian" friends, and trying to do good here and there; but they know in their hearts that there is more. Although deep down they really want it, they choose the easy way. They live their lives never experiencing the fullness God has destined for them.

The second man who hit the wall represents those people who really desire to excel in their spiritual life, but they try to advance in their own human strength. Many Christians fast, pray long hours, and busy themselves in spiritual activities to somehow tear down the wall and make it to another "level" in God. Yet they too find themselves constantly falling short. Some just give up.

The last man tries at first to climb, but then calls for the king. He initially represents the group of believers I mentioned before, but he realizes he cannot do it in his own strength. He then represents those who have a true revelation of grace. They come to a place of understanding that they can't climb the wall on their own or excel in any way regarding the Christian life without God's grace and help. When he asked the king, who represents Jesus, He swiftly answered and helped him overcome the obstacle. Now let's explore the true meaning of God's grace, so we can move forward in the life of the Spirit that lies ahead of us all.

Grace is Power

Unfortunately, many view grace as only forgiveness of sins. As a result, grace is spoken of merely as the entryway to salvation, and not the power we need to daily reign in life through Christ. Grace isn't a license to sin—*grace is our freedom from sin*. Grace doesn't only bring us forgiveness of sins; it eradicates the very entity of sin that once dominated our hearts.

How does the apostle Paul define God's grace? Because he is honored as the great apostle of grace, and rightfully so, what does he have to say about it?

> *"For the grace of God has appeared, bringing salvation to all men, instructing us to deny ungodliness and worldly desires and to live sensibly, righteously and godly in the present age...Christ Jesus...gave Himself for us to redeem us from every lawless deed, and to purify for Himself a people for His own possession, zealous for good deeds"*
>
> (Titus 2:11-14).

Here, Paul teaches that grace instructs us to deny ungodliness and to live upright in this dark world. Furthermore, he actually says that grace makes us zealous for good works. *Strong's Concordance* defines grace as "the divine influence of God upon the human heart, which has reflection in the life."[1] Everyone who has received the grace of God will reflect evidence of internal change by the Holy Spirit through his or her lifestyle. They will not be perfect or flawless in action—but they'll begin to exhibit true Christ-likeness as it's being formed within them. Grace doesn't say, "Brother, don't judge me for sleeping with my girlfriend. All is grace!" That's not grace, that's stupidity. If you truly know in your heart all that Jesus did for you to be free from sin, you would never want to touch sin again!

Grace doesn't justify sinful actions; grace longs to fully reflect the nature of God. Grace is our divine empowerment to live in the natural ways of God.

Heart Transformation

In Matthew 5, Jesus taught on the Law and highlighted the commandments of "do not murder" and "do not commit adultery," along with others. Under the old covenant, you were an offender if you outwardly disobeyed the Ten Commandments. However, Jesus took it to a deeper level by teaching that if you even hate your brother or lust after another woman in your heart—you're guilty of committing those same sins.

Jesus' goal in this sermon was to reveal that the Law commanded us to live holy lives, yet had no power to change the sinfulness that lived within our hearts. Sin begins in the heart and spills over into sinful actions. To stop us from sinning, He would have to effectually remove sin from within us first.

The prophet Ezekiel saw into the new covenant before it was ever enacted and penned these words for us to read today.

> *"Then I will sprinkle clean water on you, and you will be clean; I will cleanse you from all your filthiness and from all your idols. Moreover, I will give you a new heart and put a new spirit within you; and I will remove the heart of stone from your flesh and give you a heart of flesh. I will put My Spirit within you and cause you to walk in My statutes, and you will be careful to observe My ordinances"*
> (Ezekiel 36:25-27).

A day was coming when sin would be eternally washed away and God's creation would be thoroughly cleansed from the inside out. That day is here! When you trust in Jesus and place your life into His all-encompassing arms, something supernatural happens on the inside of you—*a Holy Spirit heart surgery.* God removes your stony heart that was unresponsive to Him and corrupted by sin's deceitfulness, and He gives you a brand new heart that is sensitive to Him, one that loves righteousness and hates wickedness (Psalm 45:7)—*the very heart of Jesus.*

That may explain why you can't sin with a clean conscience like you use to. Sin is a violation to the newness of life you've been given. Your old sinful nature is permanently removed and you've become a partaker of His divine nature (2 Peter 1:4). You are now one with Him (1 Corinthians 6:17).

After I encountered the Lord and was born again, my internal desires began to drastically change. Drug addiction fell off of me immediately, but other nagging sins took a bit more time. The Spirit of grace started to teach me personally how to live a godly life in this present evil age. No one told me to repay the thousands of dollars I stole from family and friends to feed my addictions, but the Spirit of grace that was springing up from my new nature did. I wound up repaying everyone from whom I had stolen. Likewise, no preacher told me to stop cursing, but my new spirit was not comfortable with cursing anymore. One day I was hanging out with an old friend and every word that came out of his mouth was a curse word. It didn't sit well with my spirit and right then and there I stopped cursing. On top of that, no one told me to apologize to the girls whom I had used in my previous life. But the Spirit of grace instructed me to. I sat down with certain girls and apologized for treating them like a piece of meat. I told them how loved they are by God, and they wept hearing those words of life.

Grace isn't focused on our outward obedience—*it's focused on the condition of our heart.* If Jesus can reach our heart, *the outcome will be a changed way of living.* Grace is a covenant of heart transformation—not performance orientation.

You're Holy

I use to feel unworthy to approach God when I sinned. Dirty. Hypocritical. I was attending Bible school, preaching Christ to all my unsaved friends, and pursuing full-time ministry, yet there were nagging sins that I couldn't shake. The accuser, satan would whisper into my ear, "God can't use you. You can't get it right. He'll use someone else instead of you. God is aggravated with you for your constant failings."

Little did I know at the time that God wasn't surprised or taken off guard by my sin—and He isn't with yours either. Some of the most revolutionary truths have come alive to me in the dark times of wrestling with the enemy's lies. The truth is, in and of ourselves we are one hundred percent unworthy to approach God. *But Jesus came down,* clothed Himself in our humanity, took our sin upon Himself, and clothed us in His perfect righteousness. Jesus made you worthy to approach God—and sin can't take that away from you. You are holy in the eyes of God because you've been baptized in the Spirit of Holiness. You can now stand blameless in God's presence without guilt!

Holiness is a gift from God to you. You can't earn holiness. If you could, it wouldn't be a gift. You're the righteousness of God in Christ by no merit of your own, but by the perfect merit of the Son of God. Gifts aren't earned—they are received. Jesus took on your identity as a sinner when He was on the cross so you can take on His identity as God's holy and beloved son or daughter. Because of this, you have the same right as Jesus to stand in the Father's presence as He does. His blood is enough! No sin can alter that reality. God isn't an Indian giver—He won't take your righteousness away because of your sin; He took all your sin away so He can give you His righteousness. That goes for all your past, present, and future sins. If Jesus didn't die for every sin you'll ever commit, then He'd have to come back and die a second time for all the sins He missed. He is the Lamb of God *who took away the sin of the world.* It's a done deal, sealed by the Spirit within you.

Holiness isn't only a gift from God. Holiness is the fruit of God's empowering grace working within you. The more you grasp what Christ has done for you and all you've become in Him, the more you'll walk according to your magnificently divine and spotlessly holy nature. *Holiness is a fruit of true grace.* As the Son is holy, you are holy. As the Son is loved, you are loved. In the same manner that Jesus is seated in the heavenly realm, so are you! The same access that Jesus has to the Father, you have also. You are a co-heir with Christ and a sharer in all that's His. That's the gospel!

Practicing Righteousness

It's only natural to stumble over some words in 1 John. If you're not careful, it's easy to misinterpret them. This book of the Bible is black and white—if you're an unbeliever you are of the devil, and if you're a believer you are born of God. There are no gray lines or blurry areas. Verses like 1 John 3:6 say, "No one who abides in Him sins; no one who sins has seen Him or knows Him." Wow. That's pretty straightforward. Like I said, if you're not careful and don't have a solid foundation in God's grace, it's easy to think that the apostle John is saying that born- again believers don't sin—and if they do, they don't know God after all. Take one look at any church in the world and it's plain to see that believers still sin. And if that means the church isn't truly born of God— then we're in a serious predicament.

It's vital that we see the context here so we rightly divide the Word of God. Instead of heaping condemnation or confusion, these passages should be a reason to rejoice. Let's look at 1 John 3:7-8, which is just one verse later.

"Little children, make sure that no one deceives you; the one who practices righteousness is righteous, just as He is righteous; the one who practices sin is of the devil; for the devil has sinned from the beginning."

Look carefully into the apostle's usage of the word "practice" because this is the key to helping us understand what he's saying here. If you are one who practices righteousness then you are just as righteous as Jesus is. Can you see that in the text? Isn't that's amazing? Now, practicing righteousness doesn't mean you are living perfectly all the time and never falling short. For instance, if you're practicing guitar, which means you're aiming to get better—you're still learning. You don't know everything, and surely don't have it all right. You can still play wrong notes—*but you're practicing.* Even the greatest musicians hit wrong notes from time to time. So if you are on this path of practicing to be more Christ-like, you are *just as righteous as Him*—independent of your immaturity, weaknesses, and shortcomings. Every born-again believer practices righteousness. You may falter and fail—but you don't want to. The more you believe in your God-given holiness, the more you will get better at living the holy life God has called you to.

Unbelievers, on the other hand, practice unrighteousness—and they are of the devil. They keep sinning with no desire to change, and every day they are getting better at it. Hearing this statement may be unsettling for you but John isn't holding back here. You can't serve two masters— either you serve God or the devil.

You are holy and are called to holy living; but you can't walk in the godly instructions written throughout the New Testament without embracing the enabling grace of Christ. The Christian life is impossible without the influence of His presence on our hearts.

Patience in the Process

God is bigger than your sin. He knew your failures and shortcomings before you ever committed them. He is all knowing and yet—*He still chose you.* In other words, you didn't choose Him! He knew about your porn problem, your lying issue, your selfishness, your pride, your anger, and so on. God knew exactly what He was getting Himself into when He called you by name and sealed you as His own. The Holy Spirit spoke to me when I was feeling down because of my shortcomings. He said, "Remember yesterday when you encountered Me and I poured out My love on you?" I replied, "Yes, Lord. Of course I remember! How could I forget?" He went on to tell me, "I knew how you were going to stumble today, and I still lavished My love upon you anyway. I know everything. And I love you still the same."

God isn't impatient with you—He is the epitome of patience. He isn't furrowing His eyebrow in anger because you can't get it right. He isn't disappointed with your incessant failings. In fact, He's the one offering to pick you up! He's cheering you on. He's offering all the grace you need to overcome sin's lethal grip so you can live in the beauty of holiness. You aren't holy one minute and unholy the next. You aren't the righteousness of God when you're living right, and a filthy sinner again when you fail. You're the righteousness of God, in spite of your sin—and you're learning to live righteously by God's empowering presence within you.

The Heart of Humility

Grace is a heart issue, so I want to delve into an important posture of heart that is required for living in the grace of God. The Scriptures tell us a couple ways that grace is accessed. I want to hone in on one of them here.

> "For God is opposed to the proud, but gives grace to the humble"
>
> (1 Peter 5:5).

The floodgate of God's grace is released through the power of humility! Grace is given to the humble; and those who exalt themselves will constantly feel opposed by God. Let me give an example.

Some years ago I was driving from Kansas City back to Dallas with my sister and a friend. It's roughly an eight-hour drive without traffic. But on the way home I missed a crucial turn, which wound up adding an extra two hours to our trip. Needless to say, I was peeved—and it was written all over my face. For thirty minutes I didn't say a word. I was looking at the GPS every twenty seconds, hoping that the estimated time of arrival would magically change back to normal. *Nothing.* Heaviness loomed over me, anger was boiling inside of me, and all I wanted to do was scream! Then the still small voice of the Spirit said to me, *"Son, you can keep this attitude, and this ride home will be torture for you and everyone in the car. Or you can humble yourself and turn your heart to Me in prayer."* The last thing I wanted to do was pray! I felt justified in my anger and I didn't want to change. *It was pride.* And because I was holding onto pride, nothing was working for me. I was miserable.

It wasn't easy, but I forced myself to humble my heart, look to Him, thank Him out loud, and worship Him with all I had. Suddenly, as my heart yielded to His power-packed grace—the floodgates of His presence opened wide above me. I encountered Him in such a way that everything changed. Before this encounter my life was devoid of color. Everything was dark and dismal in my hardhearted world of pride. But as soon as my heart bowed low in surrender to Him and my lips rose to worship Him, grace allowed me to see in majestic color again. Thankfulness filled my heart for the beautiful day, my family and friends, my health, and His presence. My walls of pride came crumbling down as I chose humility. Will *you* choose humility?

> *"For You do not delight in sacrifice, otherwise I would give it; You are not pleased with burnt offering. The sacrifices of God are a broken spirit; a broken and a contrite heart, O God, You will not despise"*
>   (Psalm 51:16-17).

Your tender conscience, humility of heart, and repentant attitude is what pleases God more than anything. He isn't pleased with the good works we offer Him to compensate for our sins—all of our righteous deeds are like filthy rags before Him (Isaiah 64:6). Contrary to popular belief, you don't need to punish yourself for your sin because Jesus took your punishment. You don't need to put yourself in "time out." He wants you to humble yourself and reach out to Him. In turn, the enabling grace of Christ will pour out upon you. His presence will lift you from the dust into a glorious experience of union with Him. Humility breaks the chains in your life and thrusts you into an encounter with the heart of God. The river of the Spirit rushes to the lowest place! The lower you go, the higher God takes you!

The Grand Paradox

I was a smoker for roughly six years. When I came into Christ, drug addiction fell off of me immediately, but my smoking addiction was as strong as ever. I tried *everything* to quit. Cold turkey didn't work. The patch was useless. I tried inhaling nicotine straight into my lungs to curb my addiction. I even tried smoking a whole pack of cigarettes in one sitting—cigarette after cigarette hoping that I'd make myself so grossly ill that I'd never want to touch those disgusting cancer sticks again. To my horror, that foolish idea backfired. In fact, the addiction only grew worse because my body was craving an even larger amount of nicotine than ever before! Needless to say, I felt hopeless in beating this demon. In frustration and disappointment, I sought the Lord about my struggle. I got on my knees in my room with my Bible on the floor in front of me. Crying out to God, I told Him that I couldn't do it and that He'd need to do it for me. I told Him that I'd simply keep on smoking if He didn't take it away. A few minutes later I opened my Bible and my eyes landed on Luke 18:27 (NIV), "What is impossible with man is possible with God."

Right then and there, I knew God was telling me to stop trusting in my own efforts and to fully rely on His grace. I did, and the result was freedom from my nicotine addiction. I completely lost taste for it and didn't crave it again. His grace was released as I stopped trusting in my own ability (pride) and humbled myself to trust fully in *His ability in me* (humility).

> *"Such confidence we have through Christ toward God. Not that we are adequate in ourselves to consider anything as coming from ourselves, but our adequacy is from God, who also made us adequate as servants of a new covenant, not of the letter but of the Spirit; for the letter kills, but the Spirit gives life"*
>
> (2 Corinthians 3:4-6).

I've held the above Scripture near and dear on many occasions in my life. I've often felt incompetent to serve God the way He has called me to. Many carpets have been soaked with my tears as I've poured out my soul to God. I am very aware of my weaknesses and insufficiencies' to be all that He says I am! Fear has gripped me, insecurity has rocked me to my very core, and depression has debilitated me and stolen my peace. I've been hurt, backstabbed, and ridiculed. I know what it feels like to feel led by God to do something, but say no because of the paralyzing effects of fear. Yet, through all my tears, struggles, and failures I've learned vital truths that make me who I am today. Beyond a shadow of a doubt, I've come to understand that without His Spirit in my life I am absolutely hopeless to live out my faith in the fullest sense.

Without Jesus I am nothing—yet He constantly encourages me that *in Him* I am perfect and can do all things. I will live forever in the paradox of "Jesus I need You!" and "Jesus I have You!" I will always remember that I am nothing without Him, yet I am exceedingly wonderful in Him—a supernatural phenomenon.

If you want to live empowered by God's grace, then *ask Him to teach you humility*. Ask Him to give you a soft, tender heart towards the Spirit's prodding. Ask Him to be your counselor and teacher in all things. Ask Him for a pure and clean understanding of His grace that isn't diluted with the religious rubbish so many teach today. Don't try to climb the wall on your own. There's no need for you to keep running into the same wall. And don't let your misunderstanding cause you to become complacent. Call out to Jesus—He is grace. He's all you need.

Grace Sees Who You Really Are

Before this chapter comes to a close, I want to show you a Scripture that reveals how Jesus sees things so differently than the world does. This Scripture will prove that religion is adamant about pointing out flaws while Jesus is preoccupied with restoring broken lives.

In Luke 7, a religious leader invited Jesus over to his house for dinner, which He gladly accepted. During dinner, a prostitute entered the man's home with an alabaster vial of perfume. She fell at the feet of Jesus, anointed Him, washed His feet with her tears, dried them with her hair, and kissed them over and over again. The Pharisee began to judge Jesus for not stopping this woman because she was a prostitute! Jesus discerned his thoughts and shared a parable with this man.

> *"It's a story about two men who were deeply in debt. One owed the bank one hundred thousand dollars, and the other only owed ten thousand dollars. When it was obvious that neither of them would be able to repay their debts, the kind banker graciously wrote off the debts and forgave them all that they owed. Tell me, Simon, which of the two debtors would be the most thankful? ...Simon answered, 'I suppose it would be the one with the greatest debt forgiven.' 'You're right,' Jesus agreed...This is why she has shown me such extravagant love. But those who assume they have very little to be forgiven will love me very little"*
> (Luke 7:41-44, 47 TPT).

The Pharisee couldn't see past the women's lurid past and sinful lifestyle. Jesus saw clearly into the posture of her heart, and her true repentance and humility captivated Him. The grace in His eyes emboldened her to break through this religious man's opinions to fall at Jesus' feet in loving devotion.

Others may judge you based on your past or present sins, Jesus won't. He sees with completely different lenses. He sees past your current struggle into a new creation heart that loves Him more than life. God sees the holiness of His Son within you and your desire to live right— even when you're weak and wrestling. Your humility captures His heart so much that He can't help but pour out His presence upon you. You are now free to stand before Majesty because of the grace of Christ. It becomes effortless to receive from heaven's hands and experience the bliss of His presence when you grasp His uncompromising grace towards you.

"May the grace of Christ...be with you all. Amen"
(2 Corinthians 13:14).

Chapter 8

Condemnation Free

"Do not look at his appearance or at the height of his stature, because I have rejected him; for God sees not as man sees, for man looks at the outward appearance, but the Lord looks at the heart"

(1 Samuel 16:7).

A struggle of mine over the years has been self-condemnation. The reason I use the term *self-condemnation* instead of condemnation is because it comes from me—not God. "There is no condemnation for those who are in Christ Jesus" (Romans 8:1). Since I accepted Christ, all I've wanted to do is live in a manner that is well pleasing to Him, but like everyone else, I've fallen short along the way. I believe that self-condemnation is the one of the greatest killers of divine union in the body of Christ. It is the pure-hearted sons and daughters who are victims to this slow-killing poison. Unfortunately, preachers and believers who don't truly understand the new covenant are propagating legalistic lies that are hindering many from experiencing the glory of God.

I've never once doubted God's love for me; but I have doubted His pleasure in me. Because of my apparent weaknesses, I thought God wouldn't be able to use me. I felt as if God would pass me by or choose someone else who wasn't so much of a failure. Every day I pursued Him and set the course of my life in the direction of following His will—but it was a bumpy road. Depression would loom over my head like a thick, dark cloud, and hopelessness consumed my soul like a sickness. My days often felt like a rollercoaster—up and down, up and down—until I felt so nauseous I wanted to puke.

I would scream at God, asking Him why He wouldn't free me from sins I didn't want to commit. I'd cry, I'd swear (and feel terrible afterwards), I'd isolate myself from people—yet nothing made my inner turmoil subside. There were days when I was feeling great, because in my own estimation I was living up to the high standard I had placed upon myself. Other days I'd be weighed down with heaviness because of my lack of self-control and obedience to what I thought God wanted from me. Little did I know, it wasn't the Lord being hard on me, *I was being hard on myself.*

The Devil Knows the Bible

Did you know the devil knows Scripture? When Jesus was led into wilderness for forty days, the devil came along to tempt Him. Three temptations ensued, and each time Jesus stood His ground. One thing that's important to note from this story is that the devil quoted Scripture to Jesus, trying to woo Him out of God's will. Isn't that fascinating? Today, the devil does the same thing to believers. For example, when you lie, he'll whisper in your ear, "All liars, their part will be in the lake that burns with fire and brimstone (Revelation 21:8), and if we don't have an understanding of God's Word, then we'll fall victim to the deceptions of the evil one. This Scripture is actually referring to people who aren't born again. If you read 1

Corinthians 6:9, Paul makes a similar statement. After he says that all wrongdoers won't inherit the kingdom of heaven, he explains himself by telling the Corinthian believers, "and such were some of you. But now you're washed and justified." He was telling the believers of Corinth to stop acting like those who don't have Christ. The devil wants you in the dark regarding these Bible passages. Taking Scriptures out of context is his forte. The devil will never tell you, "there is no condemnation for those who are in Christ" when you sin. He'll always whip out the Scriptures that highlight your failure and heap guilt on you for not measuring up. Get the Word of God into your heart and you won't become a victim to the devil's lies.

Condemnation is a serious killer of passion in your relationship with Christ. Your intimacy with God will be greatly hindered if you don't learn to live without the spiritual disease of condemnation. How can you draw near to God when you feel like He's displeased with you? Think about it this way: do you like approaching people when you know they are angry or unhappy with you about something?

That's a no brainer—of course not. In fact, you would go out of your way to avoid the individual. In the same way, it's impossible to boldly approach the throne of grace—like we're told to—if we think God is disappointed in us, displeased with our life, or angry because of our sins. The apostle of love, John the Beloved, said it this way:

> *"Whenever our hearts make us feel guilty and remind us of our failures, we know that God is much greater and more merciful than our conscience. My delightfully loved friends, when our hearts don't*

condemn us, we have a bold freedom to speak face-to-face with God"

(1 John 3:20-21 TPT).

If your conscience condemns you, your faith will be stifled from entering boldly into the presence of God like you should. That's why the sacred blood of Jesus was spilt for you. His blood was poured out to cleanse you from a guilty conscience so you can have bold freedom to approach the throne of your Father! The blood of Jesus speaks a better word than the blood of Abel. Abel's blood cried out, "vengeance!" because of sin, while Jesus' blood continually cries out "mercy!" for every sin from the beginning of time until the end. The writer of Hebrews explained:

"Therefore, brethren, since we have confidence to enter the holy place by the blood of Jesus, by a new and living way which He inaugurated for us through the veil, that is, His flesh, and since we have a great priest over the house of God, let us draw near with a sincere heart in full assurance of faith, having our hearts sprinkled clean from an evil conscience"

(Hebrews 10:19-22)

The truth of the matter is, Jesus was condemned on the cross, so you can live condemnation free. If God was to condemn you for your sin, He'd be dishonoring the cross and all Jesus did—and that's not an option in God's mind. Jesus was crucified for you to be justified—*just as if you never sinned.* He's loyal and committed to what He did for you. Now you have the same access to your heavenly Father as Jesus.

One day the Holy Spirit lovingly and firmly told me, "Take the boxing gloves off." At first this statement confounded me. Then He repeated it again, "Son, take the boxing gloves off." Still confused, I decided to ask the Lord what He meant. He replied, "Stop beating yourself up. The more you punch yourself, the more bruised you become. The more bruised you are, the weaker you are. The weaker you are, the more susceptible you are to fall." That was a life-altering revelation for me. As a new creation with a heart to love and please God in everything, self-condemnation is the propensity we must learn to overcome.

Think about this for a moment: condemnation reveals the purity of your heart. *How so?* you may be thinking. Well, you wouldn't feel guilty, shameful, or condemned over sin if you didn't have a true desire to live holy and pleasing to God. Before you became a believer, you didn't feel remorseful about your behavior. Since you came into Christ, you've come to hate the sins that you once enjoyed. By no means am I saying that condemnation is a good thing, but I'm offering a broader perspective. Recognize that your heart is the Lord's, and your feelings of regret and sorrow over your sin derives from a place of pure intention.

Condemnation is exactly where the devil wants you. Why? Your boldness is stolen when condemnation latches onto you like a leech. Your passion is quenched. It kills your faith. If you aren't walking in communion with God because of condemnation then you'll be more susceptible to run to sin to satisfy you. The good news is…the gospel is the power of God to live above self-condemnation and in the beauty of first love passion!

God Sees the Heart

During this time when I was dealing with self-condemnation, the Holy Spirit was speaking to me in ways that boggled my mind. He was releasing words of life into me, and my brain was having a difficult time computing them. The words of grace that dripped from His lips were setting me free to be loved, and to love more than I ever have before. It wasn't merely concepts or doctrines, it was living, active, and permeating the very core of my being.

During afternoon chapel at Bible school, we'd do one song of worship then transition into our afternoon class. This particular afternoon, the manifest presence of God was flowing so powerfully within the room that the school leaders decided to keep the worship going for an extra couple of songs. I remember like it was yesterday. I felt the heat of God flowing through my body and I couldn't stop jumping and dancing. While this was happening, my thoughts drifted off into unmentionable things. It was a full-on assault from the devil. The worst part was that I couldn't stop the thoughts, no matter how hard I fought. What really amazed me about this whole experience more than anything else was that the presence of God never left me—in fact, the intensity of His glory increased upon me in greater measure.

After the time of worship ended I walked to my seat and asked the Holy Spirit why He allowed me to experience His presence when my thought life was filled with darkness. Quickly, He answered with love and truth, *"Son, I saw past your thought life into a pure heart that wants nothing but to live in a manner pleasing to Me. You didn't want to think those thoughts. Your heart loves Me and wants to obey Me, and that's what matters most in My eyes."*

God isn't looking for an immaculate performance in His people, but a heart turned wholly toward Him. God doesn't call the perfect, because that kind of person doesn't exist—but He does perfect those who are called. We're all in process and He's more patient and merciful with us then we know.

During that time, the Song of Songs was coming wildly alive to me in the secret place. I read through it day and night as the Lord was ravishing my heart with truths of how He sees me. One particular Scripture that the Lord highlighted after this encounter I had with Him was, "You are altogether beautiful, my darling; there is no flaw in you" (Song of Songs 4:7 NIV). In God's eyes, you are altogether lovely, and there is no blemish or spot in you at all. When Father God looks upon you, He sees the beauty and holiness of His Son within you. Jesus took your sin so that you would become the righteousness of God in Him.

False Comforts

If you feel cut off from God because of your sin, your fleshly weakness will arise to tempt you into indulging yourself in the false pleasures of sin. Whether it is comfort eating, pornography, movies, a past relationship, shopping, sports, hobbies, etc.—you'll be motivated to indulge in pleasure apart from Christ. Not that a few of the things I mentioned above are evil in themselves, but it's the idolization of those things that is wrong. A friend of mine would lock himself in his room and watch movies all day when he felt God wasn't happy with him. Movies aren't evil, but the full absorption that takes place is. Another buddy of mine would run to ex-lovers when he was experiencing guilt and condemnation. Now that is never right. Regardless of the circumstance, we always have a choice in tough times to turn *to* God, or turn *from* Him.

Paul calls God the God of all comfort (2 Corinthians 1:3). Jesus called Him our Comforter. If we aren't turning to Him for comfort and receiving it in full, then, sadly, we'll run to the false comforts of this life, especially the ones that are most familiar.

Freedom from the "Have To's"

I remember I would often feel schizophrenic because one moment I'd be experiencing His loving presence, and the next moment a cloud of self-condemnation hung over my head and He felt miles away.

The Holy Spirit began breaking these chains off of me by whispering in my ear some of the most radical, transformational, and even offensive truths I've ever heard. For instance, it didn't matter where I went, I felt that God wanted me to stop everyone and share Christ with them. Don't get me wrong, there were times where He specifically led me to certain individuals to minister to them, but other times it was my inner-legalist telling me that I had to—*or else.* One time I was at the store trying to get some necessary shopping done when the battle began to rage. I felt like God wanted me to speak to someone about Him, but I didn't want to stop what I was doing. Fear and condemnation began to rush in like a flood. Suddenly, the still small voice of the Holy Spirit told me, *"If you never evangelize another day in your life, I'd love you the same. You don't need to evangelize for My approval."*

I was blown away—I hardly had words to respond. The pressure was removed and instantly I felt the light yoke of the Lord placed upon me. I know what you may be thinking, but God wasn't offering me a free pass to never share Christ again—He was setting me free from the *have-to* mentality. He was transforming my heart to live from the new covenant instead of the legalist way of the old covenant. The law said, "Obey and you'll be blessed, disobey and you'll be cursed." New covenant grace says, "You're blessed, independent of your right and wrongs— now be a blessing."

The truth of the matter is that I'm hard-wired with an enthusiastic drive to reach the lost. God fashioned it within my DNA. However, the pressure to evangelize everywhere I went was stealing this passion and paralyzing me from action. Realizing that God loves me and will never stop is a serious game changer. Coming to terms with those realities set me free and empowered me to do the very things I was struggling to do. Consequently, I began evangelizing more than before! I don't have to—*I get to.* I am free to live led by the Spirit instead of the grueling, heartless demands of the Law.

Self-Criticism

While praying one evening and offering my prayer out loud to the Lord, the Holy Spirit moved me and began to take over. Multiple Scriptures were pouring out of my mouth as the Spirit gave me utterance. The verse that captured my attention most was, "May these words of my mouth and this meditation of my heart be pleasing to you, Lord, my Rock and my Redeemer" (Psalm 19:14 NIV). Momentarily, I stopped and prayed about why this Scripture was resonating as a *now word* from God.

The Holy Spirit then ministered to me by saying, "Son, you've neglected the renewing of your mind. You're self-critical and negatively pick yourself apart. *When you're critical of yourself, those meditations aren't pleasing to Me.* And because you're critical of yourself, you're critical of others." I realized right then that God isn't pleased when I harshly judge myself. For so long I thought I was doing what was right by constantly critiquing my behavior, but nothing could've been further from the truth. God was teaching me the essential lesson to have grace with myself, and in turn, I started to effortlessly be more gracious with others. Naturally, grace became the dominant lenses through which I viewed my relationships and strangers I met. Don't get me wrong, I'm still on the journey, but progress is always found in making a conscious choice for grace in every circumstance.

I want to make a quick statement to help you understand exactly where I'm coming from. If you're an individual who is looking for any excuse to hold on tight to your sin—*repent.* Don't justify your behavior any longer. Don't play with fire. Sin will burn you badly. In the above paragraphs I am writing to the believers who yearn to live in a manner worthy of the call of God, not play in the mud with the pigs. As a genuine, godly believer, you want to live holy, and if condemnation is plaguing you, allow His grace to rain down upon your hurting heart.

"For we are His workmanship, created in Christ Jesus for good works, which God prepared beforehand so that we would walk in them"

(Ephesians 2:10).

We are God's workmanship and He created us wonderfully. He sees us as flawless and beautiful in His eyes. When God created the sun, moon, stars, animals, vegetation, and everything else, He said it was *good*. When God created Adam and Eve, He said they were *very good*. You are very good to God. No other creation of His compares to the beauty of humanity. You are the target for God's undying affection! How amazing is that truth? It's imperative that we learn to love ourselves, because God loves us. We must even learn to like ourselves, because God likes us! Stop being hard on yourself for not getting everything right; God is patient and merciful with you in your maturing process. Instead of despising God's workmanship, embrace the uniqueness of who you are and learn to love who God created you to be. Instead of trying to be like everyone else, remember that you're fearfully and wonderfully made (Psalm 139:14).

Love God, love yourself, and let Him deal with your issues. It's not your job to dissect every one of your thoughts and intentions; He's the one who judges the thoughts and intentions of the heart (Hebrews 4:12). Let God be God, and you be you. Let Him do His job, and you stick to yours. He is the Grand Liberator; your only role is to cooperate with what He's doing in you. Renew your mind to the truth, and the truth will set you free.

The Mercy Seat

Roughly six years ago I had an encounter with Jesus that changed my life. After wrestling with sin and falling flat on my face, the war with self-condemnation continued relentlessly.

One morning, I made it to work an hour before starting time. No one had arrived yet and I was alone with the Lord. As I was waiting in my truck, the Holy Spirit spoke to me, *"Put on music and dance."* Dancing was the last thing I wanted to do at that time. I struggled with God because I didn't want to obey Him. Finally I decided to yield. I blasted some music, stepped out of my truck, abandoned self, and began dancing like a lunatic before the Lord. In that very moment, I felt like king David dancing undignified before God, holding nothing back.

When the song ended I made my way back to my truck and stilled my heart and mind before the Lord. As I was meditating, His presence poured out upon me powerfully and my spiritual eyes were opened to see into the kingdom realm. The next thing I knew, I was seeing a vision of Jesus seated on His throne. He was holding a scepter in His right hand—the scepter of uprightness (Psalm 45:6). He was wearing high priestly garments, as our great High Priest who sympathizes with our weaknesses (Hebrews 4:15). His eyes were piercing my soul and He began to wholeheartedly sing a new song over me. He sang the same verse over and over again. The lyrics to the spiritual song went like this:

"I'm seated on the mercy seat, My compassion is
towards you, and My grace abounds!"

The heavenly melody and celestial lyrics were swirling around in my spirit for days and it wouldn't stop. The vision was so vivid that it kept replaying in my mind. To this day, the melody remains with me, and my memory of this encounter lives on. Seeing His eyes of mercy, feeling the bubbling emotions of His heart towards me, and hearing His words of grace impacted me in ways I've yet to fully understand. I am by no means better than anyone else who hasn't had such an encounter with the Lord, but I believe this level of experience in the Holy Spirit is possible for all who hunger for more of Him. Believe that you can go deeper in your experience of intimacy with the Lord. He will meet you in your hunger.

In the Old Testament, the ark of the Lord was placed inside the Holy of Holies within the tabernacle of Moses. In this room, the weighty glory of God would dwell in full measure. Inside of the ark were three objects: The first object was the Ten Commandments, which spoke of man's rebellion against God's holy Law. The second was Aaron's staff that blossomed, which spoke of man's rebellion against God's appointed leadership. The last item was a piece of manna that fell from heaven in the wilderness, which signified man's rebellion in complaining against God's divine provision. God commanded Moses to conceal these items within the ark by placing the mercy seat on top and sealing it shut. Not only did the mercy seat conceal these items, but if anyone were to expose these holy objects, they would instantly die (Leviticus 16:13).

Jesus perfectly fulfilled these prophetic pictures through His earthly life. He walked the earth as a man, lived the life you couldn't live, died the death that you deserved, descended into the depths of hell, and rose triumphantly to the right hand of the Father in heaven! He is now seated upon the mercy seat in heaven, receiving all who approach His throne of grace to obtain His bountiful mercy. The articles that were concealed within the ark all represented Israel's rejection of God and inability to live up to His perfect holiness. God is saying to us today, "My Son is seated on the mercy seat, covering up the sins of the world, never to be seen again. No one is to gaze upon these articles, only upon My Son Jesus and His precious blood because He fulfilled all areas of humanity's failure. Looking to these objects will only produce death, but looking to Jesus—the Obedient One—will bring forth life and peace."

There is always a picture of Jesus and His grace even within obscure passages that seem to offer a blurry view of God's goodness. When you stumble upon Scriptures that challenge your view of God's love, ask the Holy Spirit to show you Jesus within the text. Jesus is hidden all throughout the Old Testament, waiting to be found by all who hunger to see Him. Don't be exasperated by this ethereal quest. Like Bill Johnson says, "God doesn't hide revelations from you, *He hides them for you.*"[1] It's the glory of God to conceal a matter, but the glory of kings is to search it out. (Proverbs 25:2)

Shame Removed

The *Merriam-Webster's Dictionary* defines the word *shame* as, "a feeling of guilt, regret or sadness that you have because you know you have done something wrong."[2] God longs to set His people free from shame. Believers all over the world are hindered from walking in emotional freedom and joy because of shame attached to their past mistakes. Jesus hung naked on the cross, shamefully in front of His accusers, humiliated and broken, and absorbing our sins so we can be free from sin and all the shame that accompanies it.

Before I was born again, I was in an immoral relationship. The woman and I broke up after several months, but a surprise was lurking around the corner. A few weeks later the girl sat me down and told me that she was pregnant and she was one hundred percent positive that I was the father. I felt as though a train hit me and all the wind in my lungs was violently knocked out. Growing up, I always loved kids and had an innate longing to be a father—*but not yet*. It was too soon. I knew that I was irresponsible and unfit to be a dad. It turns out that she discussed everything with her mother and they agreed that having an abortion was the best option—before ever speaking with me—and they wanted me to pay for it. I didn't know what to do. I had the money, so I agreed to their decision—*and our baby was aborted*.

About a year later I got saved, and I was still gripped with shame and regret because of my foolish decision to murder my child. When I first started my relationship with God I didn't want to attend church, but my sister invited me. So I told God, "Lord, I have so many burdens weighing me down. If You kindly remove one of them in church today, I promise I'll come to church from now on." I gave the Lord an ultimatum and He had mercy on me.

I endured the whole service, all two hours of it, and nothing happened. Aggravated, I stormed off to the bathroom during the altar ministry, figuring that God didn't answer my prayer. While I was there I could hear the pastor talking through the speakers that were being amplified into the restroom. Suddenly, the pastor received a word of knowledge and said, "Someone in here is suffering with shame from going through with an abortion. Come to the altar and God will heal your heart." Instantly, I ran out of the bathroom to the double doors, but they were locked. I didn't realize that I had to go to another set of doors to get in. So I ran back to the bathroom, went into the nearest stall, sat on the toilet seat, and opened up to the Lord.

In that moment, His sweet, manifest presence poured out on me. All of my shame, guilt, and pain were removed in the light of His glorious forgiveness and love. The love of God cascaded over me like a waterfall, washing all my filth away. I left that bathroom stall a changed man—never to be suffocated by shame again.

I was at church on Father's day some months later when the pastor asked all the fathers in the room to stand up so the congregation could acknowledge and honor them. Being a single guy with no children, I didn't think twice to remain in my seat. Out of nowhere the Holy Spirit whispered into my ear, *Happy Father's Day.* I lost it! Tears came streaming down my face and I cried like a baby in response to my heavenly Father's love and faithfulness. He didn't only forgive my sin of murder, He encouraged me and gave me a hope of seeing my child one day in heaven.

A few years passed, and I was in Mozambique serving as a missionary. One night during my prayer and soaking time, I had a heavenly encounter in the Spirit. Instinctively,

I knew I was in heaven, and Jesus walked up to me holding a baby. He placed the precious child into my arms and He told me it was my baby who was aborted. He told me that it was a boy and his name is Stephen. I melted, enjoying every second of holding my son—who I will be fully united with in heaven when I pass from this world into my heavenly home.

Our Daddy in heaven goes above and beyond forgiving our sins. He restores. He encourages. He imparts hope into our hearts. It's imperative that you allow Jesus to eradicate self-condemnation, shame, and guilt from your life if you want to become more intimate with Him. Give Him your baggage and receive His life transforming grace. His words of life and love will set you free to be loved, and to love like He does.

The more you grasp that there is no condemnation for all who are in Christ, the more you'll be able to experience His life-giving presence. Ask the Holy Spirit to remove any self-condemnation, guilt, or shame that may be holding you back from entering into the fullness God has for you. Never forget the liberating truth that you are always loved and cherished by the Father, Son, and Holy Spirit, no matter what you've done.

Chapter 9

Eternal Love

"Just as the Father has loved Me, I have also loved you; abide in My love"

(John 15:9).

There are children all over the world who grow up without a father. The numbers are staggering—it's painful to even imagine. In other cases, many fathers are workaholics and are rarely ever home to invest substantial time and love into their children. This too is a tragedy. Then there are the fathers who see their children frequently, but are verbally and/or physically abusive. The brokenness that children experience when a *father or mother* treats them in this manner is unfathomable. These scenarios are incredibly damaging to the well-being of their children.

On the other hand, there are fathers who genuinely care for their kids and do their best to raise them right with love, guidance, care, and discipline. They are by no means perfect, they make mistakes too—but their intentions and actions reveal the goodness within them to genuinely play the God-given role of a parent in the life of their children. Even with these types of parents—the best of the best, the cream of the crop—none hold a match to our heavenly Father. He's the Dad of all dads! He takes the cake, and none can compare to Him.

Sadly, because we've had negative experiences with our earthly parents, we unknowingly project the image of those negativities onto our Father in heaven. In our own minds, we imagine God to be just like our earthly dad or mom. For instance, if our fathers were distant or absent, we think that God is the same way. Or if our fathers were easily enraged by our behavior, we believe that our heavenly Father is the same. Even if our parents were super strict with us, never letting us off the hook for our failures, it becomes a stronghold in our mind regarding the nature of our Papa God. An amazing Scriptural truth is that, "Though my father and mother forsake me, the Lord will receive me." (Psalm 27:10 NIV).

You don't lack a thing because you missed out on certain life lessons or experiences that you should have had as an adolescent. You don't need to let the pain of your past effect your future any longer. If your family casts you out, if your father is ashamed of you, or if your mother abandons you, the Lord—our heavenly Daddy—will gladly lift you from the ashes of brokenness and receive you into His almighty, everlasting arms.

A man who worked for my father for years once told me that my dad was ashamed of me when I was going through my rebellious stage as a teenager. Though those words weren't true, they had a greater impact on me than I thought. Years later, during a class on inner healing, the teacher asked us to quiet our hearts and ask the Holy Spirit to reveal to us areas in our lives that needed His healing touch. As I prayed, the Holy Spirit reminded me of those words that were spoken over me. I didn't even realize that I had received those words as truth and even carried that mentality into my relationship with God. So I opened myself up to Him, cried out the pain, and allowed the Holy Spirit to minister to that wound. The Holy Spirit wants to minister freedom to you with the Father's love. Every word that was spoken over you that doesn't line up with the truth of God's Word needs to be broken off and healed by the truth and ministry of the Spirit. You can ask God right now to heal areas of your heart that need His touch, and He will faithfully come to your aid and bring the freedom you ask Him for.

My Natural Parents

My mother was the one who was steadfast in her relationship with Christ when I was young. She was the glue who held our family together. When all hell was breaking loose, she'd be the one praying and believing God for the breakthrough. When I was fourteen years old my father had a radical conversion experience that turned him from a casual churchgoer into a man of God, full of zeal for the Lord. I remember wrestling with this because I felt like everyone in my family was getting saved, and I was the only one left that was semi-"normal." At the same time, I was experimenting with drugs and chasing girls—and the last thing I wanted to do was become a Christian.

Right around the time of my dad's conversion, my worldliness began to escalate and my rebellion took over full throttle. I became one of my father's first severe tests as a believer. It wasn't funny at the time, but now we laugh about the fact that I didn't make things easy on him in any sense of the word.

Being the reckless youth I was, one night I decided to take my father's truck out while I was extremely inebriated. I was on my way to a friend's house, when one of my buddies who was driving behind me decided to cut in front of me on a one lane road doing about 70 mph in a 45. The streets were sleek because it rained earlier in the day. Without thinking, in my drunken pride, I sped up, hit around 80 mph, and foolishly got in front of him. Full speed ahead, my tires lost traction and I lost control of the vehicle. I wound up hitting the car in front of me, spiraling out of control, knocking down three small trees on the opposite side of the road on someone's front lawn. The car was crushed, but by God's divine protection my friend and I left the wreck scratch-free. It was supernatural. I remembered that I had drugs on me and threw them out the window so the cops wouldn't find them—*nonetheless, they did.*

The cops interrogated me about the bag of weed they found, and my father stepped up in my defense to the officers. They told him to step aside because I was of age and they didn't need my father's consent to question me. However, my father kept pleading my case, and before we knew it we were both in handcuffs—me for drug possession, and my father for obstruction of justice. Traumatized, my mother was left in tears having no clue what to do, watching both of us being taken away by the police.

I'll never forget that night. As one of the officers walked me to my cell, I had to pass my father's. He didn't see me, but I saw him. He was sitting down, with his face buried in his hands, praying to his heavenly Father. I remember feeling like scum, knowing that I put my father through such hell—yet he still loved me and stood by my side.

I greatly appreciate my mother and father and applaud them for remaining faithful to God and loving me when it was extremely difficult and seemingly impossible at times. Because of them, I have always believed that my heavenly Father loves me unconditionally, regardless of my rebellion and sin. Even if you didn't have parents like mine, you aren't lacking a thing. Father God will father you. He will even mother you. He will be exactly what you need! Paul said he was like a mother and father to the church in Thessalonica, and God will be the same to you—but even greater. Ask Him to heal your heart and reveal Himself to you in this manner.

Our God of Burning Emotions

Statues and paintings of Jesus predominantly portray Him as angry, disappointed, emotionless, or painfully sorrowful. This common portrayal of Jesus has distorted our view of God's nature of intense love for the world. But the Bible reveals a different Jesus than the one who is often portrayed among Christians today. The Bible declares that He felt compassion for His people (Matt. 14:14), He rejoiced greatly in the Spirit (Luke 10:21), and He felt love for us (Mark 10:21). Also, the Word of God states that He was anointed with the oil of joy above all His companions (Psalm 45:7 NIV). Our God is an emotional God. He's our loving Father. He is filled with tender affections toward His children.

I'm a first-time dad to a beautiful baby girl. Before she was ever born, the emotions I was already experiencing towards her in the womb were overwhelming—*and I hadn't even held her yet.* A while back I had an encounter with God that brought tremendous healing to my heart. I saw myself as a little boy, roughly eight years old. God was there with me, my Papa, and we were running around an open field playing together. He was laughing as I jumped into His arms. I felt His love for me. I knew He was focused on me. And because of His delight in me, I delighted greatly in Him. He isn't the "godfather." He's your Father God. Daddy. Papa. He wants to heal your heart in such a way that you can feel comfortable calling Him Papa or your Daddy God.

As believers in right standing with God, one with Him in Spirit, we actually get to be partakers of His divine emotions. We get to feel what He feels. Human beings are emotional in nature, which makes sense because God created us in His image and likeness. There is nothing wrong with emotions like some grumpy preachers would like to tell you. Emotions are amoral; they can be used and influenced by light or darkness. Set your mind on sin and your emotions will be filled with darkness. Set your heart on Christ and your emotions will be filled with light and life.

Men especially have a hard time being free in their emotions. Some women do as well, but it's more prevalent among men. It's a lie to believe that women can have a closer relationship with God because they are more emotional beings. We are all emotional beings—men and women alike. Men just have a harder shell that needs to be cracked by the Holy Spirit. And when that shell is cracked, like King David, men will be able to love tenderly, worship freely, and truly embrace the gentleness, kindness, and grace of Jesus. Every believer is the bride of Christ. That scriptural truth freaks out most men, but there is a bridal revelation sweeping through the church like never before that is awakening the body of Christ as a whole to step into the burning heart of Jesus, the Lover of our souls. A loveless gospel is no gospel at all.

How Do You Hear God's Voice?

Discerning tone is critical when it comes to reading the Bible. If you don't have an intimate knowledge of the Lord, it's fairly easy to misinterpret the heart behind His words. For instance, have you ever received a text or email and had a difficult time discerning the tone the individual is using in the message? This has happened to me on multiple occasions. Sometimes it's difficult to know if they're casually responding back in a light-hearted manner, or if they're upset in some way. You see the words, but you *don't hear their tone*—so it makes it hard to discern the message. The same thing can happen with the Bible; you see Jesus' words, but you don't hear the tone of His voice and heart behind the words. He could be indifferent, angry, happy, sad, etc., but when you begin to grow in your relationship with God, it becomes easier and easier to discern His heart behind His sayings. The same goes with your friendships. The closer you become to someone, the more you will know exactly what they're saying and how they mean it—even if it's just a text message. You can almost hear their voice and tone in your head as you're reading the message.

As an example, let's look at a Scripture that I had a difficult time with for years. Here, Jesus is speaking to His disciples and mentions Judas Iscariot, who was a disciple of Christ, but would betray Him in the end.

"Jesus said to him 'He who has bathed needs only to wash his feet, but is completely clean; and you are clean, but not all of you.' For He knew the one who was betraying Him; for this reason He said, 'Not all of you are clean' "

(John 13:10-11).

If you don't have a revelation of the heart of God who desires none to perish, it's easy to misconstrue His words here. For years, it seemed to me as if Jesus was angry with Judas and took pleasure in the justice of exposing his sin before the other disciples. But as I started to grow in the revelation of God's redemptive grace, I began to hear Jesus' words differently. The tone in His voice transformed from bitter and angry to heartbroken.

As you grow in your relationship with Jesus, the simpler it will be to discern His heart—even in the most perplexing passages. You must learn to filter all the words written in Scripture through this one dynamic, monumental, biblical truth—God is *love* (1 John 4:8).

Fear of Punishment

As believers, the foundation of all revelation is the love of God. You never graduate from this cornerstone revelation. It is multi-faceted and impossible to exhaust the unlimited depths of His love towards you. If you truly want to abide in the presence of God twenty-four/seven, you must be thoroughly grounded in this revelation. Every child of God is in the process of being perfected in love. The more we understand how much He loves us, the more we will love Him in return—and the more we'll love others.

146

"We love, because He first loved us" (1 John 4:19). As we grasp His delight and pleasure in us, we'll begin to naturally and effortlessly delight and take pleasure in Him.

A Scripture I wrestled with for years was Jesus' teaching on the greatest commandments. He said,

> *"He answered, 'Love the Lord your God with all your heart and with all your soul and with all your strength and with all your mind'; and, 'Love your neighbor as yourself'"*
>
> (Luke 10:27 NIV).

Time and time again, I would read this Scripture and wonder if I truly loved God with my whole heart, mind, soul, and strength. Instead of encouraging me, it would take me down the dark road of introspection, always coming to the conclusion that I was falling short in more ways than one. Hearing so many teachers put a positive spin on this Scripture didn't help either because I knew that I wasn't living up to it and I didn't see any hope of being able to do so in the near future.

Over time, I began to understand that the commandments of loving God and loving others were still the Law. Indeed, they are the greatest commandments of all, but they are still commandments. Under the old covenant we were told to love God and love others, but under the new covenant, the love of the Spirit has been shed abroad in our hearts enabling us to love Him and others with His quality of love. It's not our love for Him that counts; it's His love for us. Jesus said, "A new commandment I give to you, that you love one another, even as I have loved you" (John 13:34).

There's the new command given by Jesus. How can we love others as He has loved us, if we don't know how much He loves us? First we must be grounded in a revelation of His love for us, then we'll be able to rightly reciprocate love to Him and those around us.

> *"There is no fear in love; but perfect love casts out fear, because fear involves punishment, and the one who fears is not perfected in love"*
>
> (1 John 4:18).

God wants to perfect His love in us. He wants to cast out all fear of punishment. I heard a sermon the other day about faithfulness to God. Overall, the message was solid, but toward the end the pastor told the congregation, "God rewards obedience for the believer, *but He punishes disobedience.*" You could hear a pin drop in the sanctuary. My heart was grieved because those words go against God's mission of perfecting us in love. He doesn't want us to fear punishment—that's old covenant—it's the inferior way and has no power to perfect us. Don't get me wrong, I believe in obedience. Obeying God should be our greatest joy. When you know you are loved by God and have a deep relationship with Him, obedience isn't burdensome (1 John 5:3). But by no means is God punishing believers for their sins. Sin has its own destructive consequences. There are times God will protect you entirely from the consequences of your sins; and there are other times He will let you reap the corruption you've sown. God knows all things, and He knows what's best for you. All is motivated by love—for God is love—and He can't be anything else.

The bottom line is that Jesus took your punishment so you can receive His reward. He bore what you deserve in His servant body, so *you* can receive all the blessings *He* deserves. That is the gospel of Christ. That is the story we need to stick to—because it's the gospel that is the power of God for all who believe (Romans 1:16).

No More Fear

Fear is the devil's greatest and most strategic weapon against the children of God. In the same way that love casts out fear, fear casts out love. Fear has the power to quench love's effect on our hearts. You can't tremble with fear and live in the love of God at the same time. We must lay our fears at the feet of Divine Love, before love can banish all our fears away. If the devil can cause you to fear, in many different ways, he can clog up the kingdom flow in your life. The Lion of Judah, Jesus Christ, is living inside of each one of us, but fear cages up this fierce Lion from being unleashed. If the devil can trap you in fear, he can paralyze you from action and from making a difference in this world for Jesus.

Learning to receive God's love will set you free from the bondage of fear. If you recognize an area in your heart that is dominated by this bondage, bring it to the Holy Spirit and ask Him to pour out His love within you in greater measures.

> *"The Spirit you received does not make you slaves, so that you live in fear again; rather, the Spirit you received brought about your adoption to sonship. And by Him we cry, 'Abba, Father' "*
>
> (Romans 8:15 NIV).

It is Christ in you crying out, "Abba Father!" The Spirit of love wants to break through all fear that fights to hold you back in life. Love is more powerful than fear. Fear is a defeated foe. Crush its head under your feet where it belongs. You don't need to be dominated by its influence any longer. The same Spirit of love that raised Jesus from the dead indwells you (Romans 8:11).

Your Worth

Jesus didn't have to come and die for us. He could have left us in our sins and sent us all to hell. Or He could have destroyed us and started fresh. Instead, He humbled Himself, put on human flesh, was tempted in the same ways we are, endured the most brutal suffering there is, and bore our sin and punishment on a criminal's cross. Why? Because He couldn't stand idly by and watch us perish at the hands of the evil one. He was compelled by holy love to rescue us singlehandedly and bring us back to our true home—*His presence.*

There's a common theme in popular movies throughout the centuries; nine out of ten have some kind of love story intertwined—if not all of them. It's common to have a movie where a young maiden is snatched away by a criminal of some kind. And there is only one person who can save her, a hero of sorts—a prince charming—one possessed by love that will stop at nothing to bring her into the safety of his arms. Why do plots like this move us so much? I believe it's because these stories tug on the deepest implanted desire God has hidden within our hearts. The evil one has captured us all, and Jesus Christ, who is Divine Love personified, our Hero and Champion, has come to our rescue to bring us into the safety of His arms. Not only that, Jesus gives us His name, His royalty, His authority and we're called to rule with Him for all eternity. The Christian life and story is the greatest epic of all time.

Christ hanging on the cross reveals to us our true worth. When humanity was robbed of its glory and trapped in satan's bondage, God determined how much we were worth by sending His Son to die in our place. Our worth in His eyes is Jesus Christ. God would never make a bad deal. He wouldn't send His priceless Son to die for inferior creatures. In the same way, when you go to the store and find something you really want, you then determine how much you're willing to spend based on the item's worth. Now, imagine this for a moment: God saw you, and said to Himself, "I know how much My people are worth—their value is equivalent to the value of My Son Jesus. I'll send Jesus into the world to buy them back from the enemy's grip." That's amazing!

For the joy set before Jesus, He endured the cross. Jesus saw your face when He was being whipped and beaten. The joy of knowing that your life was being ransomed back from the evil one through His suffering motivated Him to follow through until the end. He saw every tribe, nation, and tongue standing before the throne of God, clothed in purity and righteousness. He saw an army of tenderhearted warriors, a company of bridal lovers, a holy people called by His name as His special possession, a holy nation.

The revelation of our worth in God's eyes is staggering and nearly incomprehensible. According to Paul, God's love surpasses our ability to comprehend it (Ephesians

3:19). If that revelation is a hard pill to swallow, know that you're not the only one. It must be felt in the heart, before it can be understood in the brain. *His love must be received before it can be perceived.*

One time I was speaking with a young believer who came out of the Mennonite church. She was telling me how she felt unworthy to approach God. She deemed the Lord as so transcendent and above all, that she felt like an unworthy worm before Him. I began to open up the Scriptures to show her how God sees her and all He did to win her back to Himself to make her holy. As I was sharing these same truths, tears began welling up in her eyes and streaming down her cheeks. Right then, I saw the scales fall off. After I finished sharing, she said to me, "Michael, those words are hard to believe." She was absolutely right. The gospel is so profoundly good, so diametrically opposite to what the world and most of the church has taught us, that it can be difficult to believe at first. Yet this young girl was finally receiving the words of true life and beginning to open up to what her heavenly Father has been longing to give her: *a revelation of His heart.* Here's a Scripture that has hit me like a ton of bricks over the years.

> *"As the Father has loved me, so have I [Jesus] loved you. Now remain in my love"*
> (John 15:9 NIV, insertion mine).

In the same way that the Father loves Jesus, Jesus loves you! Imagine for a second how much the Father loves His Son, Jesus. It's impossible to fully fathom. More than that, try wrapping your mind around God loving you *in the exact same way*—it's dumbfounding to say the least.

Love Never Changes

My next statement may seem blasphemous to some, but the Holy Spirit once told me, "Son, if you kept struggling with the same weakness until the day you meet Me face to face, My love for you would never change." Hearing those words of faithfulness and commitment set my heart ablaze with passion for Him more than ever before. By no means did I use it as a license to live in sin. In fact, my hatred for sin and love for Him increased exponentially. Jesus, the Lover of your soul, is committed to you. His proposal to you was the cross. And there is no sin you can commit that He didn't carry in His body there. He *saw* all your junk. He *felt* all your sin. Nonetheless, He proposed to you—and He'll never divorce you. He's absolutely committed. Now it's time for us to remain committed to Him.

God loves you and there is nothing you can do about it. You can't sin your way out of His good graces. He's fighting for you and your purity. Nothing will make Him back down on your behalf. He doesn't only love you; *He likes you*. He doesn't like every choice you make or everything you do, but you are the apple of His eye nonetheless. Even in your foolishness, His love never changes. It doesn't matter how unfathomable the sin or gross the behavior. He's still your Daddy and He'll never disown you. A good father doesn't shun his children when they make mistakes. And He is far better than even the best father there is.

Believing in God's love wasn't too difficult for me; but it was extremely hard to believe that He liked me. Understanding that He is pleased with me and delights in my life transformed me from a striver into a lover. I use to imagine Him to be upset, disappointed, or frustrated with me when I failed. Then suddenly my failure would collide with His constant encouragement and words of life—and nothing could compare. It's been quite a journey, but every second was worth it—He's worth it. Don't give up your pursuit of righteousness (2 Timothy 2:22). Don't give up on your relationship with God, jump ship, and run to your old way of living. Plant your roots down for the long haul. When you see His face and when He pours out His manifest presence upon you in the secret place, all you endure and go through for His name and righteousness *will be more than worth it.*

Keep Burning!

While my wife and I were serving in Cambodia as missionaries, we met some of the most incredible people. A local Khmer girl who was on staff with the same mission organization shared her testimony with me one afternoon and it left a permanent mark on me. This girl was one of the first people in her local village to accept Christ, and at a very young age. Her parents were Buddhist and didn't like her newfound faith in Jesus. They often beat her and commanded her not to pray to Jesus or exercise her Christian faith. They'd even speak badly about her among the people in their village, causing her neighbors to turn on her. Some years later, her sister also came to faith in Christ. Trial and testing arose for her as well, and over a period of time she wavered in faith and slipped back into her old Buddhist beliefs. The adversity and opposition were too much for her to handle. As she told me her story, the words that stood out to me the most were, "My sister backed down when persecution came. But when my parents beat me, spoke evil of me to my neighbors, and treated me like an outcast, my love for Christ only grew stronger. My passion for Him continued to burn more than ever before!"

Trial and testing are opportunities for us to cling even tighter to Jesus. Instead of running *from Him*, let's turn *to Him*. In the Bible, the first church rejoiced when persecution came their way. When I first came to Christ, a close brother of mine said to me, "Following Jesus isn't going to be easy, but it's going to be worth it." Jesus didn't promise us a comfortable life—but He did promise an abundant life full of the nearness of His presence. In your sorrow and pain, the Lord wants to pour out the power of His presence upon you. No trial, no pain or persecution can quench this love, *if you choose to yield to His love.* Like John the apostle, lean into His chest, and receive from His heart today and forever. In the Song of Songs, Jesus sings these words over His bride, the church. Hear Jesus singing over you right now. Receive them into your heart.

> *"My love is stronger than the chains of death and the grave, all consuming as the very flashes of fire from the burning heart of God. Place this fierce, unrelenting fire over your entire being. Rivers of pain and persecution will never extinguish this flame. Endless floods will be unable to quench this raging fire that burns within you. Everything will be consumed. It will stop at nothing as you yield everything to this furious fire until it won't even seem to you like a sacrifice anymore"*
>
> (Song of Songs 8:6-7 TPT).

Your feelings may fluctuate, your circumstances may be inconsistent, but God's love is always constant. Never failing. Never fading. Never changing. Believing in God's unwavering, relentless, unconditional love is pivotal to experiencing the glory of His goodness. You must first believe it to receive it. His love never fails and His love never changes. *But His love has the power to change you.*

Chapter 10

God's Home

"Heaven is My throne, and earth is My footstool. Where then is a house you could build for Me? And where is a place that I may rest?"

(Isaiah 66:1).

Like I shared earlier, I use to be a drug junkie until I tasted of Jesus—then I became a glory junkie. His presence became the central pursuit of my life. Nothing that I had known compared to Him. Though this was true, I only experienced Him in measures. When I would desperately seek Him or spend time alone in prayer I would feel His presence, *but my heart panted for more.* Therefore, I embarked on a quest to not only experience the presence of God here and there, *but to live in the glory of His presence twenty-four/seven.* I wanted to drive my car in His presence, wash dishes in the glory, go shopping at the mall under the influence of the Spirit, and even encounter His heart while visiting the restroom. You may think that sounds nuts, but give me a chance to explain. First, let's dive into the heart of God and His predetermined plan for His beloved creation.

The Mystery Revealed

A common phrase among Christians is "God works in mysterious ways." In one sense, they are right. God's thoughts and ways are not like those that come to us naturally. Unfortunately, many cling to this truth to justify their spiritual condition instead of drawing closer to the

Holy Spirit to have God's divine secrets revealed to them. "The secret of the Lord is for those who fear Him, and He will make them know His covenant" (Psalm 25:14).

God doesn't want His people in the dark regarding His will and ways. He longs for us to come into an intimate knowledge of Him, so that we become ministers and stewards of the mysteries of God (1 Corinthians 4:1). According to 1 Corinthians 2:10, it's the Holy Spirit who reveals to us the vastness of God and all that's ours in Christ. It's in His job description to unveil the fullness of all we've been freely given (1 Corinthians 2:12). Our natural minds can't comprehend it—it must be *spiritually discerned* (1 Corinthians 2:14 NIV).

Paul speaks of a mystery that has been hidden from the men and women of old, but is now plainly published for all to see. The dark shroud of obscurity has been lifted and we've been given access into the fullness of God's predetermined plan from eternity past. What could this possibly be? Doesn't God work in mysterious ways and hide Himself from us lowly, inferior creatures? Isn't it impossible to understand God because His ways are higher than our ways? Not according to the great apostle of grace. The Lord has given us His Spirit and His Word, which are actively working to wake us up to this life-altering reality. Here it goes, the great mystery revealed:

> *"I have become its servant by the commission God gave me to present to you the word of God in its fullness— the mystery that has been kept hidden for ages and generations, but is now disclosed to the Lord's people. To them God has chosen to make*

> *known among the Gentiles the glorious riches of this*
> *mystery, **which is Christ in you**, the hope of glory"*
> (Colossians 1:25-27 NIV).

There it is. The grand mystery that God has hidden up His sleeve: *Christ in you.*

The House of God

In the beginning, God dwelt in the Garden of Eden with Adam and Eve. He walked with them closely and personally in the cool of day. There, He revealed His heart to be intimately connected with His creation. God didn't want to only be our Leader and Lord; He wanted to be our Father, our Friend, and our Companion. When our relationship with the Trinity was disrupted, throughout the Bible's narrative we see God unveiling His desire to commune with those who seek Him. Like I spoke about in an earlier chapter, God wanted relationship with Israel in the time of Moses, but they withdrew from Him and asked for law instead. In response, God gave them the Law, but He also instructed Moses to build a tabernacle where He would dwell right in the center of His people. Regardless, God's desire came to fruition in measure through the tabernacle of Moses—His presence *with them.* Everywhere the Israelites went, God's presence went also. If God moved, they moved. A cloud led them by day, and a pillar of fire led them by night. Still, the fullness of God's grand plan hadn't yet unfolded. A future day would come when God would get what He had always longed for.

Thousands of years later, Jesus hit the scene and dwelt among His fallen creation. Jesus became the living, breathing tabernacle of God wrapped in human flesh. He carried the fullness of the Godhead in His body as a prophetic foreshadowing of what He was going to reproduce in all who would believe in Him. After He thoroughly infuriated the religious leaders of His day, Christ was crucified, buried, and resurrected on the third day. He appeared to His remaining disciples and informed them of a future baptism they would undergo as the Holy Spirit would fall upon them.

Pentecost took place fifty days later, the upper room was shaken with the power of God as flaming tongues of fire levitated over their heads! The outcome was that the same people who were fearful and hiding to preserve their lives were now bravely and resolutely declaring the gospel of Jesus. Finally, the dream of God from the dawn of time came to pass. No longer was He solely our "Father in heaven," but He became Immanuel, "God with us" and Holy Spirit came to live in us. He has taken up full residence in our bodies and He now proudly and happily calls us His home—*His resting place, His holy habitation.*

I've visited many churches over the years, and I've heard a common phrase used among church leaders and believers. How many times have you heard an elder, pastor, or congregant grab a microphone and ask the church, "Isn't it good to be in the house of God today?" Listen, I'm not throwing stones here, but I believe it's important to have our minds renewed in this area. I want to really lay this point on thick. A building isn't the house of God anymore—*you are.* You don't need to attend church to encounter God or hear from Him (even though being plugged into a local community of believers is important). If you're a believer, then you carry His presence with you everywhere you go. His presence is within you, not just a portion, not even three-fourths of His presence—the fullness of Him (John 1:16). If you're an unbeliever, you don't need to run to a church building to speak with your heavenly Father—He's everywhere you turn.

In my travels, I've visited many countries where idol worship is rampant. It's common to see temples and shrines scattered throughout the territories. People gather in these places of worship, bow down, and pray. More often than not, these temples are exquisitely beautiful, exceedingly colorful, and look outrageously expensive to build. These structures are so breathtaking that the tendency is to stop and take endless pictures to capture their beauty. You can't help but pose in front of them and have a nearby tourist take pictures of you with your friends and family. Most buildings like this eventually become tourist attractions. People flock from far and wide to witness these alluring and astonishing structures firsthand. Some of the most wonderful and amazing buildings I've ever seen are Roman Catholic churches in different parts of the world. I completely understand the desire to gaze upon buildings of this nature; I enjoy it myself. But when my wife and I walk into these structures, I'm always reminded of God's eternal, unquenchable passion to be one with His creation.

Humanity is striving to build massive, elaborate, expensive buildings in hope that God will deem it worthy enough to rest His presence there. Yet, Isaiah 66:1 says this,

"Heaven is My throne and earth is My footstool. Where then is a house you could build for Me? And where is a place that I may rest? 'For My hand made all these things, thus all these things came into being,' declares the Lord. 'But to this one I will look, to him who is humble and contrite of spirit, and who trembles at My word'"

(Isaiah 66:1-2).

God has never desired to dwell in man-made structures—regardless of how pretty they are. The apostle Paul asked the Corinthian believers, "Do you not know that you are a temple of God and that the Spirit of God dwells in you?" (1 Corinthians 3:16). To you, maybe this teaching may seem elementary. Truthfully, it is. However, the church often gives lip service to this truth without ever scratching the surface of living it out practically. It's one thing to say that the Holy Spirit lives inside of you; it's an entirely different level to actually live in the power of those words of truth.

For others, this truth might be difficult to process—you view yourself as unholy and unacceptable to God because of your sins. If that's the case, beloved one, He purified you, washed away your sin, and made you an acceptable, holy home for Him to live in. Too many believers think that God is wincing and grimacing inside of them, aching to get out. That could not be further from the truth! He delights to live within you. *He chose it to be* this way! You are His heart's desire. You are His resting place. He has come down and made His home within you. In Old Testament days, the Holy Spirit would come upon people to accomplish certain assignments and He'd lift off of them when it was completed. Under the new covenant today, the Holy Spirit has made His home within believers and He never checks out. We've been upgraded from a visitation relationship to a habitation relationship with almighty God.

I love raising my hands in church because it's a picture of total surrender to God. But, if God's people aren't accurately taught, it's easy for us to imagine Him far off in the heavens somewhere instead of Christ in us, the hope of glory. I was teaching on this subject in a Bible school, and the light bulb turned on for one young man from Holland. He raised his hand to tell me, "I use to imagine God being outside of me when He spoke, but now I know He is speaking from within me, and this makes things so much more personal and intimate." Now and then, instead of raising your hands during worship, try putting them on your stomach. Imagine Jesus in you. His nearness. Oneness. This can be the single, most life-changing revelation you will ever receive if you'll let it. No matter how many times we have heard this truth, it needs to become living revelation to us.

Baptized in Fullness

The Holy Spirit has graciously and dynamically plugged you into the fullness of God. His role is to make all that Jesus accomplished for you available in your everyday life. "Now we have received, not the spirit of the world, but the Spirit who is from God, so that we may know the things freely given to us by God" (1 Corinthians 2:12). The Spirit of God is the Illuminator and Revealer of everything you've become and everything you've been given in Christ. He unveils the mysteries of the kingdom within you and compels you to cooperate with Him to see it come to fruition in your life. Because this truth is so astounding, here are a few Scriptures to prove how truly full you are in Christ.

"For of His fullness we have all received, and grace upon grace"

(John 1:16),

"For He whom God has sent speaks the words of God; for He gives the Spirit without measure"

(John 3:34),

"Blessed be the God and Father of our Lord Jesus Christ, who has blessed us with every spiritual blessing in the heavenly places in Christ"

(Ephesians 1:3).

"Seeing that His divine power has granted us everything pertaining to life and godliness, through the true knowledge of Him who called us by His own glory and excellence"

(2 Peter 1:3).

These above passages, plus many more, prove that believers have been grafted into an unending surplus of the Spirit of God to reign in this life! You don't lack the Holy Spirit, child of God. The devil would love to have you preoccupy your time with trying to earn "more of God" through self-effort and striving instead of receiving by grace all the bountiful gifts of God in Christ. The amazing news is that you've been given the fullness of the Holy Spirit and now you have a lifetime to discover and learn to walk in all that's freely yours.

From the moment you received Christ, you received the fullness of the Spirit. You may not always feel that way, but it's the truth. However, there is a second blessing that many people call the baptism or infilling of the Spirit. The word *baptize* in Greek means "to immerse, submerge or overwhelm." To be baptized or "filled" with the Spirit has to do with the experience of the Holy Spirit in your daily life. This infilling, reserved for every child of God, has to do with being empowered by heaven to infect this world with the gospel of Jesus.

Saying things to the Lord like "fill me up God," and "I want more of Your Spirit" are indeed feasible prayers, but I believe it's important for a scriptural foundation of "fullness" to be laid first. When we understand fullness, we no longer pray with a "lack mentality" but with a hunger and faith-filled confidence to walk in the fullness of what's available in the Spirit! Trying to earn "more" of the Holy Spirit through various methods of spirituality is a common deception that will only produce unceasing frustration for you.

For example, many church circles believe that after you are born again you need to "tarry" and pray extensively for an "Acts 2" baptism experience until a manifestation takes place. On the contrary, like I've said before, the Holy Spirit is received as a gift of grace through faith. No human striving necessary. Even if you didn't get "tingles" when you received, you must believe that you've received. The manifestation will come progressively.

The Sacred and Secular

Now, I want to touch briefly on an age-old heresy that has plagued the first church called Gnosticism. Understanding this will break off limitations that are commonly placed on God in the pursuit of the Spirit-filled life.

Unfortunately, this system of thought has consumed much of our Christian theology and has become terribly common among believers today also. The core belief of Gnosticism is that all things natural are inherently evil, and all things "spiritual" are holy and good. Therefore, things like wine, sex, music, and so on are considered evil or "unspiritual." I don't want to dive too deeply into this, but the Bible never rejects such earthly pleasures, instead, it teaches us moderation and to filter all things through God's Word.

One of the results of this deception is causing believers to deem time spent in prayer as spiritual, but raising a family as merely natural. Because of this, many ministers have neglected their families in their pursuit of the ministry. In doing so, they missed the glory of God that rests upon marriage and raising a family.

I want to make a bold statement here that is a direct slap in the face to the gnostic spirit: *There is no separation between the sacred and secular.*

Truly let those words sink in. *I'm not talking about the holy and the profane,* because there is a separation there. I'm talking about God wanting to be involved in every area of your life. He wants to baptize your secular with His sacred presence. He wants to show you Christ in your wife and children. He wants to pour Himself out on you while you're eating breakfast. He wants to speak with you while you're walking your dog. Invite Him into everything, do all things unto Him, and you'll find that the secular areas of your life will be swallowed up by the divine essence of heaven—His holy presence.

For years, I desired the prayer life of the generals in the faith, like Smith Wigglesworth, Kathryn Kuhlman, or John Wesley. I read their stories and teachings, and they often spoke of the countless hours they'd spend in prayer. I wanted to pray like them because I saw the numerous salvations and miracles that resulted through their ministries. While in Bible school, I spent hours upon hours in the prayer room, reading the Word and seeking God privately. Sometimes I would truly receive from God, and other times I felt as dry as an old piece of wood. I don't regret those times with the Lord; they are dear to me. To this day, I still set apart time to seek God privately. In fact, everyday I pull away with God in the secret place. It's the very desire of my heart. Yet He has taken me on a journey that has forever revolutionized the way I view prayer and worship.

In my Bible school days, a massive dodge ball tournament was going on and most of the school was attending. In my mind, it wasn't "spiritual" enough of an activity, so I determined instead to go to the prayer room. When I arrived, of course I was the only one there. I thought, *Good! More privacy for me and Jesus.* So I began to pray, and boredom hit me like a runaway train. Nothing excited me, and His presence seemed light years away.

I decided to walk by the gym and peek in to see what was going on at the tournament. As I approached the gym doors, something strange began to happen—His manifest presence steadily increased all around me. When I opened the door and stepped into the gym, I was suddenly overtaken by the love and goodness of God. Then the Holy Spirit spoke to me, *"I'm in here. I'm in their laughter. I'm in the fellowship. I'm in the fun. If you want to spend time with Me, join Me in here."*

Because Christ is within us, our time with Him isn't meant to be isolated to a prayer room or church service only. He wants us to invest in relationships, be godly parents, enjoy hobbies, etc.—and He wants us to include Him in these areas. The fact that He now lives within us, and goes everywhere we go, points to the reality that He wants to be intimate and commune with us in everything we do!

I can't tell you how many times I've felt suffocating pressure to "get into His presence" or engage in some type of spiritual activity. If I was spending a lot of time with family and friends, and not as much time in prayer, I felt as though I was falling short. Little did I know that prayer is supposed to be as effortless as breathing. It's turning our heart, setting our gaze, sharing our life with Him. Prayer is meant to be an internal conversation and inward posture of heartfelt worship to the One who is ever-present and eager to speak with us.

For example, one day I was with some friends and they were playing the guitar and making up silly, nonsensical songs just for the fun of it. I remember feeling like I needed to get alone with God and pray, instead of "wasting my time" with meaningless songs. Then out of nowhere, I felt the presence of of my Jesus fill their songs and their laughter. Holy Spirit kindly said to me, *"Son, I'm here in the silly songs, in the childlike joy, in the friendship and camaraderie. You don't need to be reading your Bible to enjoy My presence and communion. You can enjoy Me here and now."*

These are only a few examples of the many times God purposely reformed the way I view prayer. And I thank God He did! Life becomes so much more rich and full when you begin to see Him in everything and everyone. He doesn't only want to be a part of the areas of your life that look "spiritual." He wants to immerse you with His life-giving Spirit in the seemingly insignificant details of your life. He's the God of the big and the small. We shouldn't put God in a box by considering some parts of our lives more spiritual then others.

Praying Without Ceasing

"Pray without ceasing," Paul admonished in 1 Thessalonians 5:17. He didn't mean for us to spend twenty-four hours a day, seven days a week interceding for the nations. Praying without ceasing is living aware of God and communing with Him in the sacred space of your heart. It's doing all things unto Him, and inviting Him into everything you do. Some ministers brag about how much they pray, but eight hours a day simply isn't enough. *The standard is without ceasing.* God has access to you twenty-four/seven, and you have access to Him just the same. No more hindrances. You can live undone in the light of His countenance, all day, every day. Sin is gone; you are worthy to approach Him by the blood of Jesus. Take advantage of this powerful opportunity. I'm not saying it'll come easy, but I am saying that it is a reality worth pursuing. It's not impossible—this reality is within reach for all who commit within themselves to know Him.

The more you grow in intimacy privately, the more your heart will be drawn to experience this reality publicly. His presence will pour out even into the mundane areas of your life. If you're waiting at the doctor's office, begin to set your mind on Jesus in you. If you're in traffic, pop on some anointed worship music and sing to Jesus with everything you have. You won't be able to get enough of your time with Him. *Your secret place will spill over into your every place.*

When God was waking me up to this reality of constant, unhindered access to His presence, I would experience things I never had before. My daily routine was to get up early and spend an hour or more with God before I began my day. This specific morning, I slept through my alarm and had to rush to get ready so I wouldn't be late for a meeting. I quickly threw my clothes on, ran downstairs, and jumped into my friend's car. Suddenly, I remembered that I didn't think of Jesus once that morning. So I took a few seconds and began to meditate on His love and nearness. The sweet and tangible presence of God swiftly flooded my heart, and joy overtook me! I didn't pray for an hour that morning. All it took was a thought, *a moment of acknowledgment.* One second of faith before Him brought about His nearness, and those few moments in the car became my morning devotional. I received more in those five minutes than many long dry hours of forced prayer.

True Worship

Worship is far more than what most believers have a grid for. To most, worship is a slow song that you sing at church. Yes, you can consider that time of connecting and personal sharing with God as worship. In fact, worship is critical in our lives. But in this section, I want to help expand your thinking to see worship in a much deeper and broader sense. More than a song, worship is a lifestyle. Let's look at the words of Paul to gain further insight:

> *"Therefore I urge you, brethren, by the mercies of God, to present your bodies a living and holy sacrifice, acceptable to God, **which is your spiritual service of worship**"*

> (Romans 12:1).

According to this verse, presenting ourselves to God as holy sacrifices is our acceptable form of worship. In this book, I've worked diligently to teach that Jesus offered the sacrifice that put all other sacrifices to shame. This applies in regard to salvation and being right with God. This also relates to receiving all the blessings of God stored up for our lives. All is grace, and all is received by faith. We've come to understand that when there is love, sacrifice doesn't feel like sacrifice at all, yet Paul is telling us that we're supposed to lay our lives down as sacrifices. How does that line up? Let me share a story that may help you understand.

I met an older man who was extremely sick and needed a wheelchair to get around. This man spent hours each day just tending to his basic needs and daily hygiene. But no matter what was deteriorating in his body, he was always thanking and praising Jesus. A pain would shoot through his body and he'd react to the pain with a small groan, then immediately retort, "Thank you Jesus. I love you Jesus!" I committed to help him for a few days to clean his sores and bandage his legs. I remember one night when I was itching to get to the prayer room to spend time with God, and the time I was taking to help this man was being prolonged by various last-minute needs that he had. I was trying to rush through everything and *this man could feel it.*

As I bent down to clean one of his feet, I looked up at this amazing man of God and the Holy Spirit said to me, "This is worship to Me. Taking time to love and serve this man who is in need is a sweet smelling fragrance of worship before Me—a pleasing and acceptable sacrifice." God knew that spending hours helping this man wasn't the only way I could have spent my night. He also knew that I wanted to do other things, but I chose to be there anyway. That night, I didn't need to be in a prayer room on my face before Him. Cleaning the sores of one of His cherished ones brought pleasure to His heart, and I was blessed knowing that God was pleased with my miniscule sacrifice.

Jesus said in the gospels that if we feed the hungry, clothe the naked, visit the prisoner, and spend time with the ill, that we're doing those acts of mercy unto Him (Matthew 25:31-46). Ask the Holy Spirit to wash your eyes and make them full of light so you can see Jesus in everyone you come into contact with. See your King in each person you meet. When you see Christ in the people around you, it becomes easier to serve them because you see the image of your

Lover upon them. Your service will be a sweet-smelling aroma to God, a pleasing fragrance, the very essence and substance of true worship.

Some people say, "I can't forgive that person for what they've done." Exactly. *You can't*, but Christ in you *can*. Lean into Him and ask Him for the grace to forgive. Others say, "I can't love that person, he is unlovable!" That's right, *you can't*—but Christ in you can! He's given you the fullness of Him, which is all you need to live godly in this life. No more excuses. No more self-justification. Your choices and lifestyle reflect the one you worship.

Jesus poured out His life for us, now we are to pour out our lives for Him. That's why my wife and I decided to name our ministry Life Poured Out International. Jesus poured out His life for every nation, tribe, and tongue, and we want to help fulfill the desire of His bleeding heart by being His hands and feet in the world.

Focus on His Presence

It upsets me when believers are overly devil-focused instead of God-focused. They exalt the devil's "power" over the glory of God within them. It's absolutely ludicrous to be scared of the devil because he's scared of you. Why? *Jesus lives inside of you*. You have the authority of heaven backing you up. The devil fights hard to keep you in the dark of all that's yours in Christ so he can wreak havoc on you any chance he can get. The Scriptures tell us that Jesus has all authority in heaven and earth—which means *the devil has none* (Matthew 28:18).

In my travels around the world preaching the gospel, I've witnessed believers who predominantly talk more about the darkness present in the territories we've visited instead of the potential of transformation in the regions. Where much sin is, grace abounds all the more! Yes, there are demonic strongholds and evil spirits working in atmospheres God will call you too. Choose to be more aware of His presence within you then the darkness that surrounds you. You are God's home. You are a carrier of His glory. No darkness can diminish the magnitude of His light.

I love going into Buddhist temples, mosques, brothels, bars, and other places like these where darkness is prevalent and you can even feel its influence engrossing the atmosphere. Many may find those words extreme or even strange. But I've come to know that the Spirit I carry is stronger than any darkness there is in the world—not because of anything I've done, but because of what Jesus has done. With this in mind, I'll go into temples and sing songs that declare Jesus' lordship! As we worship the Lord and release His presence, we take the atmosphere back for the kingdom of light.

Instead of fighting darkness, we are to shine His light. Light and darkness cannot coexist. When the light switch turns on, darkness is dispelled. As you worship and set your gaze upon Him, His presence is poured out upon you—and in turn, you pour out His love, mercy, and power wherever you are. The outcome is that satan's work and strongholds are dismantled and the kingdom of God is established. Don't fear going into a dark place because you believe there is a hierarchy of demons there that you aren't equipped to face in battle. What a foolish doctrine! You are seated with Christ in the heavenly places, above all principalities and powers. There is no competition. The devil doesn't stand a chance. The only way he can gain the upper hand is if you don't know who you are or don't understand the authority that you carry, and if you allow fear to overcome you. In the same way that love is the atmosphere of the kingdom of light, fear is the atmosphere of the kingdom of darkness. Fear empowers satan; faith releases the power and love of God!

You are a carrier of God's glory, His majestic and holy home. The secret of the ages has been unveiled—*Christ in you.* Not only are you His home, but His presence eventually becomes the cozy, dwelling place that you call home. It doesn't matter where you are, close to friends and family or all the way across the ocean in a faraway land—His presence becomes your refuge, your hiding place, the strong tower that you run to. His presence mystically and majestically becomes the place that you feel most comfortable and safe. You are His home, *and He wants His presence to be yours too.*

Chapter 11

The Believer's Rest

"And He said, 'My presence shall go with you, and I will give you rest'"

(Exodus 33:14).

There is a realm of intimacy with Christ where striving ceases and your heart finds its rest in Him. Within this realm, all human zeal is consumed like chaff by the blazing passion of His eternal affections. As your striving comes to a close in Him, the Promised Land of His presence begins to unfold to you in ways that exceed human comprehension.

The first generation of Israelites out of slavery spent forty years in the wilderness heading towards the Promised Land. Unbelief engrossed their beings to such a degree that they never inherited the land flowing with milk and honey. Many believe that the Promised Land is a prophetic picture of heaven, but if that's the case, then the wilderness is all we have here on earth. The Lord didn't want the Israelites roaming the desert for as long as they did. An eleven-day journey became a forty-year trek, and they still didn't enter His rest. According to Hebrews 3 and 4, believers today are admonished not to follow the Israelite's evil example of unbelief. We are to seize this extraordinary opportunity of entering into the rest-life of God!

The Lord did promise Israel a land flowing with milk and honey, but the only catch was that there were enemies who needed to be overthrown in the land of inheritance. Since heaven is an enemy-free zone, the Promised Land can't be symbolic of heaven. Instead, it speaks of a reality available to everyone who is tenacious enough to believe in Jesus *here and now.* Your Promised Land is awaiting you— you can enter *today* (Hebrews 4:7). The enemy wants to hold you back from stepping into the Promised Land of the rest-life of God, but the good news is that he is already defeated, and the victory is yours. On top of that, you don't need to visit the land flowing with milk and honey, only to return to the dry, arid wilderness of unbelief. Once you taste and see, you can set up shop and take up permanent residence. There is a life far above your current experience and beyond your wildest imaginations! God's rest is awaiting your faith response.

The Noise of Life

The world is running around a thousand miles per hour, while Jesus is patiently waiting in the stillness, beckoning you to come,

> *"Come to Me! Are you weary, carrying a heavy burden? Then come to Me. I will refresh your life, for I am your oasis. Simply join your life with Mine. Learn My ways and you'll discover that I'm gentle, humble, easy to please. You will find refreshment and rest in Me"*
>
> (Matthew 11:28 TPT).

An invitation has gone out from the throne of our heavenly Father asking you to slow down and answer His call to come closer than you ever have before. Drawing near is precisely what you need, and the one thing most people avoid because they have "a lot of work to get done." Jesus, the King of the world and the Creator of heaven and earth is inviting you to find your rest in the safety of His lovingkindness. He wants to fill you to overflowing with His Spirit. Draw near to Him with sincerity and faith—and the miracle power of rest will flood your soul!

A God Kind of Striving

Countless believers struggle to live in the rest of God on a continual basis. Frenzied, we run the rat race of life, struggling to find Jesus in the midst of our constant busyness. We may momentarily visit this resting place under the shadow of His wing, later to retreat back into bondage to the cares of this world. Overwhelmed and anxious, we strive to become successful, prosper financially, grow our ministries, and so on, but in doing so, we reclaim the role of "god" by taking the wheel in our lives, instead of trusting in Jesus.

In Hebrews 4:11 we're exhorted to strive to enter the rest of God. Why strive? Isn't that the opposite of rest? Doesn't God want to liberate us from striving? Yes, He does, but the striving referred to in this verse isn't a striving according to our human flesh. Human zeal cannot produce the might of God. The apostle Paul is referring to the empowering grace of God's presence within you.

"Not by might nor by power, but by My Spirit,' says the Lord Almighty"

(Zechariah 4:6 NIV).

"For this purpose also I labor, striving according to His power, which mightily works within me"
(Colossians 1:29).

It is *His* power that must be working in and through you, not your human effort. The Holy Spirit is working diligently to teach you how to rise above the chaos of life so you can enter into your God-ordained rest. Trust is the key in this elaborate equation. Trusting=resting. This trust isn't founded in your own works of righteousness, instead, it is in all He's done and what He's doing in you. Hundreds of voices are yelling in both of your ears every day, drowning out the voice of your King. Every day, the noisy static of the natural world and the tyrants of hell are silencing the voice of your Beloved. Will you allow these influences to steal your peace? Or will you determine to trust in Christ with all of your heart?

Media tells you one thing, family members tell you another, church leaders teach something else—who can we trust? Ultimately, in God's Word we can trust—we can confidently anchor ourselves in His unchanging Word. I'm not going to sugarcoat the truth here: choosing to trust Jesus with your whole life isn't always going to be easy—but the outcome is rest for your soul and joy inexpressible and full of glory (1 Peter 1:8)!

The Reality of Living "In Him"

When talking about the believer's rest, people automatically think of physical rest. Yes, physical rest is important and you should try it sometime. It works—seriously. But the rest I'm speaking of is far more than taking a nap, working five days a week instead of seven, or sleeping for eight hours each night. The believers rest is a *spiritual rest*. For example, one man can be hard at work on the railroad yet possessed with an internal peace that cannot be shaken. While another man can be vacationing in Puerto Rico, lounging on the beach, but stressed out and anxious about his business back at home. Spiritual rest is intrinsically connected to the level of our trust in God, and above all else it's an internal condition.

Allow me to share with you some powerful truths about your identity that should stabilize you in the grace of His rest. As a believer in Christ, your position is *in Him*. And in Him, *it is finished*. Jesus defeated *every* foe (sin and death), dethroned satan, and eternally stripped his authority away; and has granted you the same divine destiny, nature, and authority He possesses. Nothing is impossible for you because Jesus lives within you. All things are under your feet. You don't need to be subjected to the dark powers of this age any longer. Whatever belongs to the kingdom of darkness has no legal right to touch you. Heaven's reality is at your fingertips. To be more precise, *heaven's reality and atmosphere is within you.*

> *"He has accomplished for us the complete cleansing of sins, and then took His seat on the highest throne at the right hand of the Majestic One"*
>
> (Hebrews 1:3 TPT).

No one is greater. No throne is higher. He is above all. He overcame the world and sat down victoriously. Satan's been stripped of all authority, and all authority in heaven and on earth belongs to Jesus Christ (Matthew 28:18).

"Far above all rule and authority power and
dominion, and every name that is named, not only
in this age but also in the one to come"
(Ephesians 1:21).

If Jesus is seated on the highest throne at the right hand of the Majestic One, above every power and authority, then where do you think you are seated, child of the Most High God?

"God has raised us up with Christ, and seated us
with Him in the heavenly realms in Christ Jesus"
(Ephesians 2:6 NIV).

Understanding this has the power to change everything. You are seated with Christ in the heavenly realms. Christ isn't fighting a battle in heaven—*the war is already won.* He is seated in victory, *and you are co-seated with Him* above the powers of this age. By God's gracious gift, you've become a partaker of His triumphant victory. Your body may be walking on the ground but your spirit is one with heaven's fullness, face to face with the Lamb of God. If this is true—which it is—that means you are seated above the power of sin, death, the devil poverty, sickness, trauma, fear, depression, religion, and so forth. Jesus has opened up a clear access point into the triumph of heaven. He's closed the door of Adam's disobedience and all that came in with it, and brought you into the full repercussions and rewards of Jesus Christ's perfect obedience. Hallelujah! Depression isn't your portion. Addiction is under your feet. Sin has lost its sting. Poverty is a lie from the mouth of satan. Jesus has become your eternal sufficiency—your all in all.

In Christ, Jesus' record of perfection is your record of perfection. In Christ, Jesus' dazzling and holy nature is your dazzling and holy nature. In Christ, Jesus' joy and peace is completely yours. All of heaven's blessings have been lavished upon you, never to be taken back. You may be thinking, *All this is fine and dandy, but that just hasn't been my experience brother. My life has been rough, and nothing ever goes my way.* I don't doubt the validity of that statement, but faith doesn't trust in past experience, faith anchors in God's unfailing Word. I'm here to say that you don't need to live under the power of the world's system any longer. It's time to take God at His Word and fully immerse yourself in the inheritance that's yours in God's Son.

My Call to Rest

During my time in Bible school, I didn't work a secular job. I saved up a large sum of money before attending and devoted my time to seeking God, building relationships with godly believers and joining various ministries, especially in the area of evangelism. My encounter with Jesus was a lot like Paul's Damascus Road experience. One minute he was chasing down believers to arrest and possibly have them killed, the next moment he was radically preaching the gospel to the same people he once ran with. While in the world, I was fully in. And after I encountered Christ, I was fully in also. No fence-riding or blurred lines. If it was Jesus, I wanted it, plain and simple. The fact of the matter is, my desire to live a life pleasing and worthy of the call of God was quite evident. I spent countless hours on my face in the prayer room and was known as the "prayer room guy." Whenever corporate worship was taking place I'd be at the front worshipping God with everything I had. If there was an outreach to go on, I was there. If I wasn't engaging in some type of spiritual activity, I was spending time with other people who were on fire for God.

Throughout the school year, anointed men and women would come to minister to the students. One week during my third semester, a children's minister with a powerful prophetic gift prayed for me. The word he released hit me like a ton of bricks. He said, "God sees your zeal and passion for Him. He loves how you love Him. You're His warrior and you will be used mightily of God. But He wants you to *learn His rest*." Surprised by his last sentence, I didn't know what to think. *Wait, what? Learn His rest? I didn't come to Bible school to rest! Men and women of God who possessed power gifts put serious work into it. They prayed for countless hours, interceded constantly for the lost, and they evangelized everywhere they went. I want to be used mightily too Lord! Doesn't rest mean taking more naps, praying less, and cutting back on evangelizing? This guy must have missed it*, or so I thought.

After my frustration subsided, I shrugged it off and moved on with my day. Later on in the afternoon, I went to help a spiritual mother of mine, who is extremely prophetic as well. The next thing I knew, she looked me straight in the eyes and said, "The Lord says, you're His warrior, and He loves your zeal and passion—*but He wants you to rest*." At this point, I started to get a little freaked out. "What's the deal with this *rest* word?" I asked God. A day or so passed by with no clarity from the Lord.

The following day, I woke up early and went to breakfast in the cafeteria. A close friend of mine was there, so I sat to eat with her. Like usual, I rushed through my meal to move onto whatever spiritual activity I had lined up for the day. She stopped me and spoke directly, yet lovingly, "You're an awesome man of God, a warrior in His army, but the Lord wants you to *learn His rest*." My jaw dropped as I gave her this blank look, awkwardly responded, "Thank you," and walked away slowly. My mind was blown. It wasn't prophecy that freaked me out. I was familiar with prophecy and was surrounded by people who naturally flowed in that gift; that wasn't the issue. It was this haunting word that I couldn't seem to escape.

Thankfully, over time I realized God didn't want me to stop everything I was doing. He was reaching into my very core, the seat of my deepest perceptions and motives. God wanted me to do life from a place of intimate rest in Him, instead of religious duty or rigid obligation. Lovingly, God was turning my attention and affection on Him and away from my performance-based mentalities.

Garden Works

Before the fall, Adam and Eve were given a clear mission from the Lord. The nature of this mission wasn't passive in the least bit. The garden wasn't created for Adam and Eve to swing in hammocks all day and frolic with animals from morning to night. In fact, in Genesis 2:20 you see Adam partnering with God by naming all the animals and the birds in the sky. Adam and Eve's mission was as follows:

"God blessed them and said to them, 'be fruitful and increase in number; fill the earth and subdue it. Rule over the fish in the sea and the birds in the sky and over every living creature that moves on the ground"

(Genesis 1:28 NIV).

The assignment God called Adam and Eve to wasn't menial. They were placed in a garden that needed tilling, and their bodies had a God-given capacity to be strong and work hard. Which means they weren't created to sit around and sing worship songs all day. They were created for work—*good works.*

Today, in many church circles, the term "good works" is treated as foul as curse words. To many, you're considered a legalist for encouraging your people to engage in good works. But the apostle Paul—who carried a clear and pungent revelation of God's grace—believed otherwise and saw its value. Let's look at a few verses below:

"This is a trustworthy statement; and concerning these things I want you to speak confidently, so that those who have believed God will be careful to engage in good deeds. These things are good and profitable for men"

(Titus 3:8).

"For we are God's handiwork, created in Christ Jesus to do good works, which God prepared in advance for us to do"

(Ephesians 2:10 NIV).

"And let us consider how to stimulate one another to love and good deeds"

(Hebrews 10:24).

Mankind was created to labor with the Lord, empowered by His divine life. Dead works can be defined as anxious toiling in your own human strength in effort to earn something from God that is already yours in Christ. Good works are the fruit of a person's life who is abiding in the love and grace of Jesus Christ. There is a huge difference. One is flesh, and one is Spirit. One is God, and one is not. We were never meant to operate solely out of our God-given abilities without God's living influence. His Spirit is our life source and without Him we can do nothing of eternal worth. Before the fall, Adam and Eve were living empowered and fueled by God's holy influence upon their hearts through intimate fellowship with the Trinity. This is what I like to call *garden works*, or *good works*. This is bearing fruits of righteousness through the revelation and knowledge of who we are now in Christ—blameless, flawless children of the Most High God.

After the fall, everything changed drastically. Adam and Eve ate from the tree of the knowledge of good and evil, even though God explicitly forbade them. Consequently, He dished out punishments for their actions, but what I want to zero in on is the punishment of Adam.

"Cursed is the ground because of you; in toil you will eat of it all the days of your life. Both thorns and thistles it shall grow for you; and you will eat the plants of the field; by the sweat of your face you will eat bread, till you return to the ground"

(Genesis 3:17-19).

In the first couple chapters of Genesis we see Adam working alongside the Lord, yet remaining in constant unhindered fellowship with Him. However, when the trespass entered in we suddenly see a whole new order being established. Adam once labored *with the Lord,* and *in the Lord's* strength tirelessly, without one drop of sweat rolling down his brow. Work was effortless for him—no strain or fatigue was involved whatsoever. His work was done with sheer joy and bliss. Now he will have to strain himself with tedious labor to provide food for his family. And the same goes for all the generations that would follow him.

Thorns and thistles represent the curse of sin. When Jesus was going to the cross, He wore a crown of thorns, signifying that He took away the curse of sin once and for all. God told Adam that by the sweat of his face he would eat bread. When you start to sweat, it begins to roll down the crown of your head and trickles down your brow. Likewise, Jesus wore a crown of thorns on His head. Drops of blood soaked His forehead and dripped down His brow, revealing to His people the full lifting of sin's curse through His shed blood. Because of Jesus' finished work you can now experience the fullness of God's blessings and favor. You can work *in the Holy Spirit* and be more fruitful than you've ever been on your own. Jesus can get done in one minute more than you can do in a lifetime. Lovers get more done than workers in the long run. Learning to rest in Christ is essential to bearing spiritual fruit for the kingdom of heaven. Lovers of God stay active in the Lord's work—never becoming apathetic—yet remaining plugged into the presence of our faithful God. His presence amply supplies all the fuel necessary to accomplish the mission He has set before us.

Thus far, we've concluded that the believers rest is available to everyone who is daring enough to actually *trust completely in Him instead of their self-effort*. Also, this same rest isn't physical but spiritual in nature. Finally, we've come to see that God wants His people to be empowered through relationship with Him to such a degree that true lovers of God will accomplish more than the religious crowd of our day. Let's go even deeper in our definition of God's rest by elaborating on a key element found in the book of Exodus.

True Rest

A core Scripture for me when I think of God's rest is Exodus 33:14. The Israelites were constantly bickering, complaining, and refusing to trust in the power and character of God Almighty. This boggles my mind, considering He just delivered them from the hand of their Egyptian oppressors. Not only did He deliver them, He did so with His strong hand, demonstrating that He is the God above all gods. Yet they continued to ungratefully trudge through the wilderness, complaining against God and His ways. At this point, Moses lost his patience with the Israelites and began to plead with God about His people. The Lord responded,

> *"My **presence** will go with you, and **I will give you rest**"*
>
> (Exodus 33:14).

Notice the emphasis I added into the verse. You can see God's correlation with His presence and the rest He was promising Moses. When I saw this, my heart leapt with exuberant joy. *God's presence is the source of our rest.* His nearness instills rest into the fabric of our souls.

The rest of His presence was the substance of the Garden of Eden, the very atmosphere that permeated every inch of space. All activities were done not by the might of man but by the life-breath of God. Do you think the Lord broke a sweat when He created the galaxies, stars, and planets by simply speaking a word? What about the mountains, landscapes, or vast oceans spread across the surface of the earth? Of course not! He effortlessly wove the awe-inspiring tapestry of all things without any resistance whatsoever. It wasn't until the fall that humanity's relational tie with God was severed in two. Separation anxiety set in, the glory of humanity faded because of their lack of union with the Light Himself, and suddenly the fears of life took their throne within the core of our beings.

How can this rest be restored after it's been lost? That's where Jesus came in. He came in Person to bridge the gap between humanity and our heavenly Father. "For God is one, and there is one Mediator between God and the sons of men—the true man, Jesus, the Anointed One" (1 Timothy 2:5 TPT). Therefore, we can confidently and unreservedly declare that Jesus Christ is our Sabbath Rest. He forever bridged the gap of sin's separation and carried us back into the Father's glory, never to leave. The very moment He ratified the new covenant in His precious blood, rest was released and made available to all who fix their gaze upon the Perfect One and all He's done. Forgiveness of sins is now ours in Christ, sin's barrier and curse has been obliterated entirely, and the wall of separation forever removed.

> *"And now you must repent and turn back to God so that your sins will be removed, and so times of refreshing will stream from the Lord's presence"*

> (Acts 3:19 TPT).

Peace in His Presence

The peace that Jesus pours into our hearts surpasses our ability to mentally comprehend it (Philippians 4:7). The world can't give you the same quality of peace that Jesus can—it's otherworldly (John 14:27). The peace of Christ is what enables you to remain unusually calm in the midst of difficult and life threatening circumstances (Mark 4:35-41). Jesus doesn't only give you peace—*He is your peace.* His presence is your peace. His presence is your rest. He is the Giver of peace and He is peace itself. *He is the Giver and the gift.*

Beloved, peace is your inheritance—it was paid for in full for you to enjoy. Anything less is a rip-off from the evil one. The devil shakes in his boots over one Christian who walks in the peace of Christ. The peace of the gospel is part of God's armor that we're called to put on (Ephesians 6:15). When you walk in peace, you trample the head of satan under your feet.

Just like rest, peace doesn't come to the passive. Everything in this world is fighting to steal your peace. You must stir up spiritual fortitude and seize the promise of God that's available to you. You must determine in your heart to live in peace, or else you'll live your Christian life without it. Here's a Scripture that has fueled my passion to possess His peace in every given situation in my life.

> *"But he was pierced for our transgressions, he was crushed for our iniquities; the punishment that brought us peace was on him, and by his wounds we are healed"*
>
> (Isaiah 53:5 NIV).

One of the very reasons Christ endured the horrific suffering He did was for your soul to be filled to overflowing with His peace. Christ paid the highest price to set you free from depression, anxiety, stress, worry, fear, and every form of darkness that steals your peace and rest in Him. Peace begins with a choice. You must choose to no longer be a victim, and to arm yourself with the mentality of a victor. The kingdom of God within you suffers violence, but the violent ones take the kingdom by force (Matthew 11:12). The violence this Scripture speaks of has nothing to with earthly weapons and physical fighting. This verse is talking about a spiritual violence—refusing to tolerate what Jesus died for you to be free from.

He'll be your peace that surpasses understanding. He'll be your heavenly peace that can be found nowhere else but in Him alone. Peace is a fruit of the Holy Spirit (Galatians 5:22), and His Spirit lives within you. It is not out of reach. It is not far off. It is not in the clouds somewhere. Peace is within you—Christ in you the hope of glory (Colossians 1:27).

Rest and peace go hand in hand. When you learn to trust Him in all things, peace and rest flood your soul. Without the rest of His presence, our hearts will be discontent and always searching for more.

Rest is the result of the faith-posture of your heart engaged with the presence of God. God desires for you to enter into His presence. The good news is that you can enter and never leave. Regardless of what you're going through, draw near to Jesus and stay plugged into the presence of God.

"Thou hast made us for Thyself, O Lord, and our heart is restless until it finds its rest in Thee."
—St. Augustine of Hippo

Chapter 12
Soul Wholeness

"And do not be conformed to this world, but be transformed by the renewing of your mind"
(Romans 12:2).

Some have claimed that the great sculptor Michelangelo, when speaking of his crafting methods, said this:

"In every block of marble I see a statue as plain as though it stood before me, shaped and perfect in attitude and in action. I have only to hew away the rough walls that imprison the lovely apparition to reveal it to the other eyes as mine see it."

Within the slab of marble, Michelangelo saw a statue hidden inside. All he had to do then was chip away anything that wasn't the statue to bring forth what he saw in his innovative mind. In the same way, God is the Master Sculptor and we are His piece of marble. God sees who He created us to be long before we ever manifest its reality. Latent within your born-again spirit is your true identity—*the real you*. Holy. Blameless. Powerful. Christ-like. However, God is in the process of chiseling away every area of your life that doesn't reflect this glorious truth through the working of the Holy Spirit and His transforming grace.

Christianity isn't about becoming something that you're not, it's about un-becoming everything you were never meant to be. We're discovering who we really are and learning to walk out our true nature in Christ. As you begin to understand who you are in Him, the Holy Spirit begins to strip away everything that wasn't supposed to be you in the first place.

All of us have had the world's perspectives and philosophies define us in one way, shape, or form. Perhaps your family and friends told you lies that you carried as a heavy load upon your back since childhood. Maybe it was the dominant religious teaching of your Sunday school teacher who has skewed your image of what Christianity is actually about. Either way, it is time you let God's opinion define who you truly are, and lay all others aside. This is what the renewal of the mind is all about. It's rejecting the lies you've been fed, and embracing the truth of Christ. You aren't becoming holier as the days go by; you're discovering how holy Christ has made you by His precious blood. You aren't getting more of the Spirit through your various spiritual disciplines; you are drinking in and experiencing more of the Spirit's fullness that you already possess. "Do not be conformed to the ways of this world, but be transformed by the renewing of your mind" (Romans 12:2).

Renewing the Mind

In our discussion about abiding in God's presence, I must take the time to teach on the renewing of the mind and the multi-dimensional arena of our soul. You'll find yourself living a defeated Christian life with no presence or power if you don't take these things seriously. When lies occupy your heart and mind about who you are and who God is, they act as a barrier between you and the Lord.

I want to share an illustration I heard John Bevere use in one of his sermons, and add a slightly different application. Imagine this:

> You were born to a king and queen in rich royalty. The day you were born, you were kidnapped by thieves and taken far away into the darkest region of your country. For twenty years you were forced to cook, clean, and be a slave to these evil and treacherous kidnappers. Your good and loving king and father sent out search squads for those twenty years, relentlessly looking for you. Finally, after all that time, one of the squads found you and took you back to the palace you were always destined for.

> On your first day home you wake up early, go out to the pasture, and find cows to milk. Next, you go to the chicken coop, get some eggs, and walk to the kitchen to start cooking breakfast. A servant walks in and says, "No, no! Please stop. You don't make breakfast. We serve you. Here in this palace are the finest chefs in this county to cook for you, and we have people hired to take care of the animals. You're the royal son; this is not your responsibility." You comply, "Okay, okay, I'm sorry."

> After breakfast you now go to your room and you start to wash your clothes in the bathtub. The next thing you know, the maid walks in and stops you saying, "Please stop, that's our job! You don't need to do these things. You are the royal heir, we serve you." You reply, "Okay, okay. I'm sorry."

Just like the king's son in this story, we've been taken captive by the evil one, and it was the unceasing, loving pursuit of our Father-King who brought us back home. But now that we're home, there is just as much to unlearn as there is to learn. The world has trained each of us to think like slaves instead of children of the King of kings. When you come into the kingdom of heaven, it's pivotal that you allow the Holy Spirit to renew your mind so you can live like the kingdom son or daughter you are. You are no slave—you are a royal heir of God's kingdom. But in this kingdom, you don't rule with an iron rod, forcing your authority on others and demanding their service. Instead, you rule with a towel in hand, washing the feet of your fellow countrymen and laying down your life for the overall benefit of others.

What you believe greatly affects your emotions and behaviors. When your thought life is governed by lies, feelings like depression, fear, anxiety, hopelessness, and discouragement take control of you. As a result, you don't live according to God's perfect and pleasing will. Similarly, when your thought life is governed by God's truth, feelings of peace, joy, love, happiness, and gratefulness well up from deep within you. Whatever you believe, materializes in your life. That's why Paul and Silas were able to sing praises to God while locked in a prison cell. They refused to allow hopeless thoughts to fill their minds; instead, they set their gaze on Jesus—who is the Truth—and sang songs of praise to Him who is worthy! The outcome was supernatural breakthrough. Not only for them, but all the prisoners around them were also set free.

Every feeling and action is attached to a deep-seated belief system. Growing up in a broken world with messed up philosophies about God, humanity, and the purpose of life inevitably form our perceptions and worldviews. God passionately wants to tear down all beliefs and strongholds of the mind that are in direct opposition to the truth of His kingdom. If you want to change the way you live, first you must change the way you think.

Repentance is the process in which your mind is renewed. Many mistakenly think repentance is a one-time ordeal, when instead, *it is a lifestyle.* Don't listen to preachers who nullify the importance of repentance. At the same time, it is critical that we rightly define it, because many have distorted this powerful word. Repentance isn't what many ministers have made it out to be. When hearing the word *repentance,* many believe that you must grovel on the floor before the Lord, cry out for hours, and roll around in sackcloth and ashes to earn God's attention. The good news is that you already have God's undivided attention. His eyes are always locked on you. Repentance doesn't turn God back to you—repentance turns *you* back to God. In other words, repentance isn't about changing God's heart toward you—it's about changing your heart toward Him. In its simplest form, *repentance* means to change the way you think. "Re" means to do something again. "Pent" is the root word in "penthouse" which refers to a high place. God wants us again and again to turn away from inferior ways of thinking onto the higher reality of God's kingdom. God wants us to see everything through His lenses. We can't afford to have one thought in our mind that doesn't line up with God's eternal, unchanging Word. This is only possible because we have the mind of Christ in our born again spirits (1 Corinthians 2:16).

Identity Truths

Here I want to briefly list some scriptural truths that every believer should be firmly established in.

- **You are justified** (Romans 5:1), which means God sees you just as if you had never sinned. It's time to see yourself the same way.

- **You are the righteousness of God in Christ** (2 Corinthians 5:21), which means that when God sees you, He sees the perfect righteousness of His Son within and upon you—not your apparent sinfulness.

- **You are dead to sin** (Romans 6:11), which means you no longer have a sinful nature living within you, you have become a partaker of God's holy, divine nature (2 Peter 1:4).

- **You are blessed** because God will never hold your sins against you (Romans 4:8).

- **You are accepted by God** (Ephesians 1:6) and you were **chosen by Him** (John 15:16) before you could ever choose Him.

- **You are one with Jesus** (1 Corinthians 6:17).

- **Your body is His holy temple** (1 Corinthians 6:19).

These are only a few of the countless Scriptures that reveal how God sees you. It's time to stop judging yourself solely on the natural, and lay a strong foundation of God's Word in your life. You may not feel like these truths apply to you based on your current level of experience; but we are called to live by faith, not sight. Beloved ones, may the Word of Christ richly dwell within you (Colossians 3:16). When it does, your intimacy with the Lords will grow in leaps and bounds!

Father of Lies

The devil is the father of lies, and he's been a murderer from the beginning (John 8:44). His mission statement is to steal, kill, and destroy (John 10:10). The devil doesn't have any real authority, so how does he go about accomplishing his mission? The only way for the devil to gain access into a believer's life—or anyone's life for that matter—is our agreement. That's why Paul tells us not to give the devil an opportunity, meaning an inroad into our lives (Ephesians 4:27). The fall of man is a perfect example of his strategies. Satan lied to Eve, she agreed with his lies and Adam did nothing. They acted according to satan's deception, not the command of God. Thus, sin and death entered the world.

It's hard to imagine how many lies we believe on a regular basis. Agreeing with satan's lies empowers darkness to have its way, while agreeing with the truth of God's Word empowers light to have its way. God is constantly working to persuade us of the truth, which produces in us fruits of righteousness, while the devil is constantly working to persuade us of his lies, which in turn produces in us fruits of the flesh.

That's exactly why the devil fights vehemently and tirelessly to keep believers ignorant of their identity and authority in Christ. And if you *do* know your identity and authority, he fights to keep you from exercising it. For instance, let's say you're an undercover cop, dressed in regular everyday clothing, but you still possess all the authority that's necessary to take down a criminal. You're following a crime and happen to catch your suspect in the middle of the very act, and there is no way they can get around it. Now, you can do one of two things. You can do nothing—which would be foolish. Or you could exert your authority and take the criminal down. Like this scenario, many believers have an understanding of their authority in Christ, yet they don't exercise it when the opportune time arises because of fear and intimidation.

It's crucial that we stop being controlled by the lies of the devil, and begin to live by the truth of God's Word. But how can we live by the Word, if we don't know what it says? We must dig into the treasures hidden in the Scriptures, chew on His words, ingest them, and take prayerful and practical steps to living them out. God and the devil are both after your agreement, *who will you give it to?*

Divine Imagination

God gave us an imagination for a reason. He originally created it to be the playground where He can commune and share life with His people. He wanted it to be a place to dream with Him. I call it the divine imagination. God will often show you pictures, or visions to reveal something to you, and He'll use your holy imagination as the vehicle to get His message across. If I ask you to close your eyes and imagine a juicy cheeseburger, I bet you're able to do it. Now, if I ask you to imagine it, but this time to keep your eyes open, you'll still be able to do it. It's because the imagination is your inner-eye or spiritual eye. It's how you were created to see, *even without seeing with your physical eyes.*

In the same way, God can communicate to us through our imagination, and so can the devil. The Bible calls these vain imaginations. The devil has perverted this beautiful gift from God and takes the opportunity to sow lies, fearful images, and perverted thoughts into our minds in an effort to control us. That's why we must guard our hearts and be particular with what we allow into the gate of our eyes. Images can remain with us for decades if we aren't intentional about renewing our minds in those areas. Whatever vain thinking we're prone to, it's of utmost importance that we heed the Scriptures and take those thoughts captive to the obedience of the Word of Christ (2 Corinthians 10:5)!

The Garden of the Soul

The words *soul, heart,* and *mind* are often used interchangeably throughout Scripture. Often these words are used to speak about the multi-faceted arena of our soul. Our mind has to do with our thoughts, and our heart has to do with our emotions. Both are intrinsically one within our souls. You're a three in one being, like God is three in one. You're a spirit being, you have a soul, and you live in a body. Therefore, your mind and heart are woven together as one entity within your soul.

Our souls can be compared to a garden, and this garden needs some serious work. The Holy Spirit is the Master Gardener. The more we grow in intimacy with the Holy Spirit and allow Him to teach us the truth of God's Word, our souls are progressively being transformed into a lush garden where much fruit can grow and thrive. The Holy Spirit's job is to pull up the weeds and thorns that choke away our divine life and to plant truth within us so new life can grow.

> *"You must catch the troubling foxes, those sly little foxes that hinder our relationship. For they raid our budding vineyard of love to ruin what I've planted within you. Will you catch them and remove them for me? We will do it together"*
>
> (Song of Songs 2:15 TPT).

We have a large role to play in renewing our minds, but we don't do it alone. It is a divine and sacred partnership. We work together and cooperate with the Holy Spirit to remove all that hinders intimacy, and to plant all that pertains to kingdom living. The devil will let a fox loose to try and spoil the work that the Spirit has done within our hearts. With the Spirit's help, we're to discern the demonic activity and catch the intruder before real damage can be done. Let the Holy Spirit have His way in you. Let Him pull up the bitterness, shame, pain, and lies that have squelched His life from flowing freely through you. Be intentional in your prayers about giving Him everything that interferes with your love relationship and spiritual maturity. God is passionate about your mind being renewed and your heart being healed so He can take you higher and deeper into glory encounters that will forever radically change your life.

Healing our Hearts

In the same way that our minds need to be renewed, our hearts need to be healed. The key to being healed is facing the pain head on and allowing Holy Spirit to come and bring the healing and comfort that you need. Some people are unwilling to face their pain; they'd rather bottle it up in hopes that it'll one day fly far, far away, never to be seen again. The truth of the matter is, *it won't*. It will remain with you and dictate the way you live until it's fully dealt with through the grace of Christ and work of the Spirit.

I recently heard a testimony of a young preacher who had pride issues growing up. His father wasn't around and at a young age he had to take a fathering role in his family. Because of his upbringing, he became the kind of person who steamrollered over people, always desiring to be the strongest, greatest, and most dominant person in the room. He hurt and agitated a lot of people in the process. When he got saved, his issues persisted. He was clearly anointed by God and became a powerful preacher, but his relationships suffered because of his internal wounding. Noticing this trend in his life, he prayed about it and asked God why people didn't like him. The Holy Spirit then told him to envision every scenario where he was hurt growing up. Baffled by this response, he didn't know where to start. Still, he conceded. Next, the Holy Spirit told him to imagine every time he hurt and offended others. Again, he was confused and overwhelmed, but he conceded. By the time this was through, hours had passed and he was wondering why God would put him through something so grueling and painful. The cross then suddenly appeared before him, and he witnessed Jesus dying for all his offenses and offenders. Divine love poured into his heart and freedom came to him.

You must be proactive in your relationship with God. Don't let issues be swept under the rug. Bring them to Him, and He'll mend your brokenness. Cooperate with the Holy Spirit. Let Him minister to the dark places that you conceal from even the ones you love the most. Let Him rub the healing ointment of His love and mercy on the raw and tender areas of your heart. All wounds are meant to heal. Even the natural order of things reveals this spiritual truth. When we cut ourselves physically, our wounds heal naturally over a period of time—they heal especially fast when treated properly. But if we don't treat them, there is a chance of infection. Once infection sets in, it takes longer for the healing process and can be quite painful, long-term damage can even occur. Deal with issues quickly as they arise, and it'll take less time for you to heal in the long run.

Jesus said, "Blessed are those who mourn, for they shall be comforted." (Matthew 5:4) Sometimes crying is the only reasonable response when facing pain. All that we've bottled up over the years will need to come out one way or another. Many feel stupid or pathetic crying over past hurts. I want to tell you that there is no shame in crying—or weeping for that matter! There have been times I've been offended and hurt at God because I didn't understand why circumstances unfolded the way they did. At first, I didn't realize I was offended until the Holy Spirit highlighted it to me. I remember one time specifically when I was crying and screaming out, "I'm mad at You, God! I'm mad at You!" with everything within me. Tears were running down my face, and my heart was receiving the medicine of His grace. People hate to cry, yet tears are an outward manifestation of an inward reality. Tears reveal the inward work of the Spirit in an outward fashion. It's okay to cry—that goes for men too. God created you with tear ducts also, not just women. Don't be afraid of letting God into your darkest and most hideous secrets. God's a big boy—He can handle it! He knows what you're thinking before you speak it, and He knows what happened before you ever disclose the information, so no holding back!

"You perceive my thoughts from afar"
(Psalm 139:2 NIV).

"The Word of God is living and active...and able to judge the thoughts and intentions of the heart"
(Hebrews 4:12).

He knows the baggage you carry, the trauma of your pain, and the brokenness you can't seem to mend. He knows you better than you know yourself. Vulnerability and transparency are vital in your relationship with the Holy Spirit. He is the Comforter and the Healer of your soul. As you invite Him into your thoughts and emotions that need His healing touch, He will speedily come with His transforming grace and soothing love to make all things new. When your heart is whole, you begin to live out who you truly are in greater measures. Hurts and pain rob you of living life to the fullest, as God intends.

I've heard many ministers teach that God wants to break us. God doesn't want to break us—*He wants to heal us.* Jesus came to bind up the brokenhearted (Isaiah 61:1). Don't allow bad teaching to infiltrate your thinking. See what the Bible says about everything. Don't just receive every word a pastor or teacher says. Test it with the Word. He takes your broken and contrite spirit and applies the healing balm of His presence generously to the areas where it's needed.

Beholding and Becoming

"Beloved, now we are children of God, and it has not appeared as yet what we will be. We know that when He appears, we will be like Him, because we will see Him just as He is"

(1 John 3:2).

As we gaze upon Him in the secret place, we are transformed into His very image. As we encounter Him in intimate prayer, we are changed from the inside out. It is important not to misinterpret this passage. In spirit, you already just like Him. You are as righteous as He is. You are clothed in His spotless innocence. You are blameless and holy before Him in love. But you're not fully living up to these powerful realities. As your mind is renewed by the Word of God, your experience in Him becomes even greater. You approach Him with unequivocal boldness and seek Him more enthusiastically because of His outlandish goodness. You go deeper in prayer because you understand your access to Him. As your mind is renewed, you are able to enter into a fuller communion with Jesus, and His presence is more real and tangible to you. Encounters with the Lover of your soul become normative when your belief system aligns with the truth of God's unfailing Word. The Bible admonishes us to fix our eyes upon Christ, and behold Him. The more you see Him and the more you commune with Him, the more you will be conformed to the very image of Christ in thought and action!

"And we all, who with unveiled faces contemplate the Lord's glory, are being transformed into his image with ever-increasing glory, which comes from the Lord, who is the Spirit"

(2 Corinthians 3:18 NIV).

When the Law of Moses is read, a veil remains over our eyes, but when we turn to Christ, the veil is removed. When your heart believes the lie that you need to "do this" or "do that" to be right with God, earn His love, or enter into His presence, then the blinders of unbelief veil your spiritual eyes. But when you realize your need for Jesus, and return to Him, you're able to see His glory unrestrained and experience the unparalleled beauty of His manifest presence. Today, you have access to see His shining glory, and when you see His glory, *you'll reflect His glory!* Check this Scripture out:

"But I say, walk by the Spirit, and you will not carry out the desire of the flesh"

(Galatians 5:16).

I love this Scripture because it gives keen insight about living in the divine nature and life of the Spirit. For believers, myself included, the struggle with sin has everything to do with what we're predominantly focusing on. Many believers try to overcome sin by focusing on dying to sin. However, focusing on sin, even dying to sin, only reaps death (Romans 8:6) and isn't the key to experiencing freedom in Christ. This Scripture doesn't say, "Die to sin, and you will walk in the Spirit." Instead, Paul is telling us to focus on the Spirit and the outcome will be sin losing its power over us. Your ticket to experiencing the glory of His presence and the freedom available to you is learning to set your focus and gaze completely on Jesus in all circumstances of life. Fill your mind with the Word of God, turn your affection and attention toward Him, and the glory of His kingdom reality will become manifest to you!

Commit to having your mind renewed. You must become steadfast and persevere in this holy work. Commune with the Holy Spirit and ask Him to bring up any areas in your heart that need His healing ministry. May the Word of Christ richly indwell you, and may Christ be your firm foundation all the days of your life. Behold Him daily, and as you do, you'll reflect His glory!

Chapter 13
Practical Spiritual Living

"This book of the law shall not depart from your mouth, but you shall meditate on it day and night, so that you may be careful to do according to all that is written in it; for then you will make your way prosperous, and then you will have success"

(Joshua 1:8).

My goal for this chapter is to dive into some of the scriptural truths and practices that have helped me grow in experiencing and living in the presence of God. As you practice what's in this chapter, don't be discouraged if it's difficult at first. Our minds have been thoroughly trained to be fixated on the natural world around us. Because of this, our minds need to undergo some extensive spiritual discipline.

Going to the gym or exercising in any way has never been my forte. Some people love it, but I don't enjoy working out in the least. Deep down I know I should, the desire is there—but I always find something else I could do with my time. The same goes for prayer with many. You know you should, you even want to—but prayer gets sidelined by your favorite TV show, your many responsibilities, or time with people you love.

Another thing I struggle with when I actually start working out is that I can't even get halfway through my routine without my body screaming adamantly, "No! Stop it. Just go home and eat a sandwich." I've also noticed this take place when it comes to prayer. Our bodies are so use to waking up, being active, getting on our phones, eating breakfast, and heading to work, that any diversion—especially a spiritual diversion—is opposed by our bodies and minds. We immediately think of the ten things we could be doing and our minds wander helplessly away into oblivion.

Just like chiseled abs and pronounced pecks don't happen overnight, a vibrant, fulfilling, intimate prayer life takes time as well. God isn't the barrier we need to get past; it's our undisciplined mind that isn't accustomed to engaging with the Spirit. Don't get discouraged if you don't see instant results or have dynamic encounters right away. Keep at it and don't lose heart. You're working towards a glorious new way of living.

Today's world is all about instant gratification: if our food isn't fast food, our internet isn't high speed, or if our shopping can't be done from a smart phone—we simply don't want it. My intention isn't to knock these luxuries, I enjoy them myself—*but everything in life isn't meant to be instant.* This is especially true in the kingdom of God. I know, that doesn't sound like good news. We want everything handed to us and right away, but God has other plans. There is glory in the waiting and perseverance.

Becoming Heavenly Minded

There is no formula to experience and live in the presence of God. I'm simply giving you tools to tap into already established spiritual realities. The world has hardened our hearts toward being heavenly minded, and the Holy Spirit wants to radically change that. There are tools that God has given us to aid our pursuit of living in the fullness of kingdom realities. Until we become intentional about being a spiritually minded company of people, we won't truly mature as believers. We'll remain fleshly and carnal instead of becoming mature sons and daughters of God. Above all else, we are spirit beings. When you die, your body goes to the ground, but your spirit goes to be with the Lord. You are a spirit, you live in a body, and you have a soul. Therefore, it's critical that you learn to move past your five senses and live like the spiritual beings God has created you to be.

The Lorica of Saint Patrick says, *"Christ with me. Christ before me. Christ behind me. Christ in me. Christ beneath me. Christ above me."* These beautiful words are absolute truth, but sadly, it's easy for our minds to wander from being constantly aware of this reality. Over and over, Paul exhorted believers to set their mind on heavenly things, not earthly things. He passionately taught that believers should be a spiritually minded, heavenly focused people. He didn't warn us of being "overly spiritual." In the same way, he didn't say, "Don't be so heavenly minded that you're no earthly good." Phrases like these are unbiblical. I believe the more heavenly minded we become, the more earthly good we are. I understand that there are extreme cases of people with their head so in the clouds that you can never have a normal conversation with them. I meet these kinds of people all the time! But phrases like the ones I quoted above negatively condition believers into a hardheartedness toward the supernatural realm. Matter of fact, the apostle Paul instructed us to be spiritual in all things. By no means, did he mean for us to be strange for the sake of being strange. Nor did he tell us to put on a show to look spiritual in the eyes of others. The truth of the matter is, too many believers live so naturally that they hardly recognize or acknowledge the spiritual realm at all. Here are a few biblical examples of Paul's exhortations:

> *"While we look not at the things which are seen, but at the things which are not seen; for the things which are seen are temporal, but the things which are not seen are eternal"*
>
> (2 Corinthians 4:18).

> *"Set your minds on things above, not on earthly things"*
>
> (Colossians 3:2 NIV).

> *"Finally, brethren, whatever is true, whatever is honorable, whatever is right, whatever is pure, whatever is lovely, whatever is of good repute, if there is any excellence and if anything worthy of praise, dwell on these things"*
>
> (Philippians 4:8).

Spiritual disciplines are absolutely paramount for believers. Just because you are under the new covenant of grace, does not mean you're free from walking in the ways of the Spirit, as prescribed by the Word of God. All spiritual disciplines are for this reason, and this reason alone: "fixing our eyes on Jesus, the author and perfecter of faith" (Hebrews 12:2). These activities recalibrate your heart's attention from the things of this world

214

unto Him who is "…eternal, immortal, invisible, the only God, be honor and glory forever and ever. Amen (1 Timothy 1:17). Prayer is getting face-to-face with Him. Fasting is setting aside time to look into His eyes. Speaking in tongues is a means to detach from the natural realm and arrest our attention on the inner life of the Spirit.

Throughout the remainder of this chapter, I'm going to expound on some basic scriptural disciplines you can begin to incorporate into your prayer life that will enliven and enrich your intimacy with Him exponentially.

Speaking in Tongues

There are a wide range of subjects that revolve around the vastness of the Holy Spirit and being filled with the Holy Spirit. If you've never been baptized in the Spirit, flip to the Appendix at the end of this book. I encourage you to read that first before you continue on in this section.

I want to talk specifically about speaking in tongues. This gift has greatly benefited my spiritual life and I know that it will do the same for you. There is a growing staggering number of believers who have received their spiritual language, yet use it rarely—if ever. These believers are missing out on an explosively powerful tool God has given them to grow in the Spirit.

When I encountered Jesus for the first time, I was filled with the Spirit simultaneously, but I didn't speak in tongues yet. I remembered hearing my mother speak in tongues when I was young, so I approached my parents to inquire about it. They instructed me that the gift is for anyone who wants it and informed me of the scriptural benefits to this wonderful gift. I asked them how to receive it, and they told me, "It's like receiving a present on Christmas day. You reach out your hands and grab it—simply receive."

I immediately raced to my room, fell to my knees, and asked God for the gift of tongues. I reached out my arms to heaven in prayer, and I spoke in tongues by faith. Holy Spirit didn't seize control of my tongue and force me to speak. *I spoke by faith.* I determined to speak in tongues as often as I could because I believed in the many benefits my parents informed me of about the gift. I'd pray in the Spirit at work, in the car, the shower, and before I went to bed. At first, my mind would resist this practice. The devil would try to convince me that I was mimicking my mother's prayer language. My mind would be flooded with lies like, "You're speaking gibberish. You sound like a fool. It's not the language of the Spirit—you're just parroting your mother."

Refusing to give up, I faithfully kept speaking in tongues on a regular basis, and about a week later my prayer language started to change. Instead of the same syllable over and over, it seemed as if I was speaking fluently in an unknown language. It began to flow out of my spirit like a river! Since then, I've never doubted this tremendous gift. Don't let the devil deceive you into not speaking in tongues. He hates tongues because he can't understand what you're saying. It's a sacred and intimate language between you and God. Not only that, it is a strategic language that can be used to shift atmospheres and release God's authority into circumstances!

The apostle Paul—who wrote most of the New Testament and is remembered for his great apostolic ministry—was thankful that he spoke in tongues more than anyone (1 Corinthians 14:18). If tongues were invaluable to the apostle Paul, then we would do well to give it a place of importance in our lives too. Here are some benefits to praying in the Spirit as outlined in the Scriptures:

1. Your spirit is praying, not your mind (1 Corinthians 14:14).

2. You edify yourself (1 Corinthians 14:4).

3. The Spirit of God intercedes according to God's will through you (Romans 8:26-27).

4. It builds your faith (Jude 1:20).

5. You speak directly to God and the devil doesn't understand (1 Corinthians 14:2).

Disciplining yourself to pray in the Spirit is a wonderful way to become more spiritually minded. In doing so, you are redirecting your focus from the natural to the spiritual. You are trusting that your spirit is praying perfect prayers, even if your mind isn't comprehending what you're saying.

Pray in the Spirit as frequently as you can to grow spiritually. You don't need to shout out loud. You can mutter under your breath or pray in tongues internally. Like the apostle Paul says, I pray in tongues more than everyone you know! At first, it may seem foreign to you—but over time you'll learn to be grateful and cherish this free gift that comes from the Father.

Reading the Bible

I have emphasized this subject throughout in this book, so I won't say much in this section. I only want to give a few practical tips. You may be thinking, *C'mon, Michael. Isn't this elementary?* You are absolutely right. If you've spent any length of time in church or were raised with believing parents, it's understood that reading your Bible is paramount to the Christian life. Yet I've met countless believers who rarely pick it up on a weekly or monthly basis, let alone a daily basis. So for the record, *read your Bible!*

Here are some practical tips that will enrich your time in the Word. I strongly recommend that before you start reading, ask the Holy Spirit to awaken the eyes of your heart and impart understanding to you. Ask Him to saturate your time and to reveal Jesus in the text. You can put on some anointed worship music and sing songs of adoration to Him before you jump into your reading. Starting with worship will tenderize your heart and escort you into His glory-filled chambers. As you set the gaze of your heart on Him in worship, stillness will wash over you from your head to your feet. As you feel released to move on from this place, ask Him where to start in the Word—then listen for His response.

As you open your Bible, don't read it merely to understand concepts and perfect your doctrinal stances. Read to know your Creator and Father. Open it up with expectation of receiving a word from heaven. He wants to illuminate the Word and teach you about His kingdom. Leave your intellect at the door—all God wants from you is a soft, open, and receptive heart to implant the good seed of His Word.

I'm so grateful that the first encounter I had with God came through His Word. When I opened the Bible and sought

Him, He spoke clearly and vibrantly from the Scriptures. From this, I learned to open the Bible with expectation to hear from Him, not merely build up my knowledge.

Even if your Bible time seems dry and boring, know that your spirit is being fed as you ingest the Word—whether you feel it or not. *That is faith.* The Bible is a supernatural book.

Praying the Word

Incorporating the Word of God into your prayer life is a key component to experiencing the fruitfulness you are destined for. If you don't learn to incorporate God's Word in practical ways, you'll find that doubt-filled prayers will flow out of your mouth—and those prayers don't avail much. Everyone desires a flourishing and fruitful prayer life, and anchoring yourself in God's Word is the vehicle that takes you there.

You'll find that when the Word of God isn't the foundation of your prayer life, you'll pray things like, "God, be with us today," or "God, make me holy in Your eyes." Prayers like this won't get you anywhere. Why? Because they have been already answered! God is with you always, in fact, His name is Immanuel, "God with us" (Matthew 1:23). And, He's already made you holy by His precious, innocent, shed blood—there's no need for Him to do it again. Imagine praying out loud like this, "God, I know You are with me. You've made me holy and acceptable in Your beloved Son, Jesus. You love me with an everlasting love. Your Spirit lives within me and I have all authority in Your name." As you speak those words of life over yourself, you're actually declaring your God-given identity. As you speak the truth of God's Word, faith is being infused into your soul to usher in a manifestation of these truths. Hebrews 4:12 declares that the Word of God is living and active, and sharper than a double-edged sword.

When you pray God's Word, you can be confident that you're praying God's will. And whatever you pray according to His will comes to pass (1 John 5:14). As you go throughout your day, sing His Word, encourage others with His promises, and pray it over yourself. Even if you don't see instant results, keep planting the seed of His Word, keep watering that seed, and wait for God to cause the growth (1 Corinthians 3:7). He always does.

Meditation Prayer

Selah is a breathtaking word found in the Scriptures. It means to pause, ponder, or reflect on the beauty and vastness of God. *Selah* is a musical term that is used in the book of Psalms for musical direction or transition. Dr. Brian Simmons, the lead translator of *The Passion Translation* expounds on this magnificent word,

> "The Hebrew word *Selah* is a puzzling word to translate. Most scholars believe it is a musical term for pause or rest. It is used a total of seventy-one times in the Psalms as an instruction to the music leader to pause and ponder in God's presence. An almost identical word, *Sela*, means a massive rock cliff. It is said that when Selah is spoken that the words are carved in stone in the throne room of the heavens."[1]

This word has very special meaning to my wife and I. Before we ever met, God spoke to both of us separately about a little girl that we'd have in the future and that her name would be Selah. When we were getting to know each other, Selina (my beautiful wife) told me about this God encounter she had and it blew me away. God spoke to both of us, and gave us our little girl's name, before we ever met! Her middle name is Gloria, which means glory. She's our promised baby, and she'll be a constant reminder to pause and reflect on the glory of God—even in the craziness of life.

To "selah" is to meditate on God. Meditation, unlike false religions, isn't about empting your mind to reach a state of nirvana—it's about filling your mind with truthful thoughts of God. In Scripture we're told to meditate on God's Word day and night. We're always meditating on something throughout the day; why not try the Word of God? Instead of meditating on the many bills you have to pay and reaping anxiety and fear, try meditating on how our Father in heaven is our Jehovah Jireh— the world's greatest Provider.

Meditating on God is one of the many ways you experience the glory of His presence. As your thoughts are fastened upon Him, the presence of God begins to manifest for you to bask in and enjoy.

Soaking

Soaking, as many call it, is a style of prayer that has become my favorite over the years. When I pray, my tendency is to pace back and forth, and it's typically very hard for me to sit still. Over the years, I've come to realize that most of my prayer time consisted of speaking in tongues, singing songs, speaking the Word, and so on—with very little listening time. Listening is an art that we'd all do well to excel in. Man can't live off of bread alone, but off of every Word that proceeds out of the mouth of God (Matthew 4:4).

During the time when God was instructing me to learn about His rest, I felt impressed to practice silence and listening in prayer. At first, this was a serious battle. I would put on some calming worship music, place a mat on the floor, and lie on my back with my eyes closed, trying particularly hard to focus and meditate. Some days I'd either fall asleep or I'd go nearly insane because of my inability to stop my racing mind from thinking about the busy details of life. But I persevered, and over time I truly began to enjoy and receive from this time with the Lord. The peace and rest my soul would feel was astronomical. The beauty of His presence was like pure, refreshing water to my soul. There were times when I would feel His presence resting on my body like a blanket, and warmth covered me from my head to my feet. As my soul was locked in on Him, it became easier and easier to hear His voice, see visions, and receive impressions from the Spirit. The most enriching prayer times I've had were simply sitting at His feet and listening to His words.

As you rest in His presence, your soul is being revitalized, rejuvenated, and strengthened. Those who wait on the Lord and rest in Him will gain new strength to run the race (Isaiah 40:31). You'll begin to notice that you feel stronger, more equipped, and ready to face your daily challenges as you learn to receive from Him in the secret place.

When you learn to still your heart and hear from Him in private, it is amazing how it will begin to spill over effortlessly into your daily activities. I started to notice that I was able to hear from Him more clearly while I was out shopping, hanging out with friends, or spending time with family. Learning to commune with God in the sacred space of your heart is an invaluable spiritual lesson that has the power to transform the way you do life.

> *"He says, 'Be still, and know that I am God; I will be exalted among the nations, I will be exalted in the earth'"*
>
> (Psalms 46:10 NIV).

Start incorporating silent times of meditating and listening into your devotions with the Lord. Fasten your gaze upon Jesus and allow His presence to wash over you. Lie at His feet and receive the words that flow from His mouth. Let His presence intoxicate and rejuvenate you. Stay with it and don't grow weary. Over time, you'll grow to love your times of soaking in the glory of His presence.

Casting Your Cares

At first, when you practice being silent before the Lord, you may notice your mind is racing in several directions. I've struggled with this myself. The apostle Peter helps us understand how to overcome this battle by telling us to cast all our anxieties on God because He cares for us (1 Peter 5:7). Before you rest in Him, it is critical to clear your mind. Whatever is looming over your head or occupying your thoughts—release it into the hands of Jesus. He'll gladly take it from you. You never have reason to fear or fret when Jesus is your Lord. Clearing your thoughts by casting your cares on God will bring you the peace you need to reflect and meditate on Him in the secret place. Peace is the optimal state of being in order to receive from the Lord. Without peace you wont be able to hear God's voice or be led by the Spirit properly because of your cloudiness of mind and heart.

> *"Praise to the Lord, to God our Savior, who daily bears our burdens"*
>
> (Psalm 68:19 NIV).

God is a big man—He can handle your baggage. Your burdens aren't burdensome to Him. He carried the sin of the world and He wants to bear your everyday burdens as well. They may be too heavy for you, but they're as light as a feather to Him.

Thanksgiving and Praise

> *"Enter his gates with thanksgiving and his courts with praise; give thanks to him and praise his name"*
>
> (Psalm 100:4 NIV).

We gain access into the courts of God by praising and thanking Him. Why? Like I mentioned earlier, as you set our mind on God, it brings us into an awareness and manifestation of the presence of the Lord. Faith in Jesus is your sacred access into God, and as you thank and praise Him for all He's done and who He is, your faith shoots through the roof! Thanking God refocuses your eyes onto what you have in Christ instead of what you don't have in the natural. In doing so, you become enraptured by the beauty and glory of all He is! Praising God shifts your heart onto the majesty and wonder of all He is from the temporal circumstances of life.

Thanksgiving and praise are both weapons we have against the schemes and attacks of the devil. If he's trying to heap fear and anxiety on you because of your less than favorable circumstances, it's time to make a choice to praise God for who He is! Begin to thank Him for all He's done in your life. As you do so, the grip of satan will be loosed and the freedom of Christ will take over.

Instead of constantly complaining about what you don't have, try thanking God for what you do have. Instead of letting depression and misery get the best of you, praise your way into the victory that is yours in Christ!

My intention in this chapter is to give you tools to keep your heart engaged with the presence of God at all times. There was no way to cover everything, but these exercises have greatly benefited me, and I pray they will benefit you as well as you put them into practice. Our hearts are so prone to wander from the simplicity of communing with Him. May we be a people who are lovers of His presence, heavenly minded, and continually abiding in Him until the day we see Him face to face.

"I worshiped Him the oftenest that I could, keeping my mind in His holy presence, and recalling it as often as I found it wandered from Him. I found no small pain in this exercise, and yet I continued it, notwithstanding all the difficulties that occurred, without troubling or disquieting myself when my mind had wandered involuntarily. I made it my business as much all the day long as at the appointed times of prayer; for at all times, every hour, every minute, even in the height of my business, I drove away from my mind everything that was capable of interrupting my thought of God."

—Brother Lawrence[2]

Final Word

My prayer is that this wouldn't just be another book, but a tool to draw you into a deeper more intimate relationship with the Trinity. All it takes is one taste of the real Jesus and you'll forever be ravished by His love. All it takes is one Word from His lips, and your heart will burn with eternal passion. Just one touch and you'll be transformed into a lover of His presence. Open your heart to Him, beloved one. Ask Him to awaken your spiritual eyes to see Him in all His glory and matchless splendor. May you be completely undone by His radiant majesty!

He's awakening His bride, the church, by the power of the Holy Spirit to step into the magnitude of all that's hers in Him. He's bringing forth an end-time army who will release and establish His kingdom, even in the darkest regions of the earth. He's bringing forth maturity in His people, that we may shine forth the fullness of Christ. It's time for His sleepy bride to rise and shine! It's time for us to take hold of God and commit to never letting go. May His glorious presence lovingly unravel you daily, as you set your face like flint towards Him and His kingdom purposes.

I pray that the eyes of your heart would be enlightened to know His everlasting love, the glory of His grace and the abiding presence of His Spirit in every situation in life.

Conclusion

Before I end, I want to give a short exhortation that I believe will be helpful for you in your journey into the beauty and power of the Spirit-filled life.

In their pursuit of God, many people chase manifestations instead of drawing near to the God who floods our human experience with His manifest glory. While writing this book, God told me to make it clear that His presence cannot be contrived or manufactured. You cannot conjure up an encounter or spiritual experience with God. Don't turn intimacy into a work; it's not a means to a greater end. You can't conjure up or produce His presence through any of your efforts. The supernatural realm has always been available and is in our midst. The angels in heaven cry out, "Holy, Holy, Holy, is the Lord of hosts, the whole earth is full of His glory" (Isaiah 6:3). Because the earth is already full of His glory, let us give ourselves to becoming more deeply personal and intimate with this King of glory with unbridled hunger and tender surrender. Every true warrior in God's kingdom is first and foremost a lover of Jesus. May you draw near to Him and learn to live in first love passion all the days of your life. In doing so, you'll go from glory to glory as the Lord takes you on the most exciting and breathtaking journey into the depths of His heart and fullness of His purposes.

"Whoever has ears, let them hear"
(Matthew 11:15 NIV).

Appendix
Baptism of the Spirit

If you're reading this section, it means you are a born-again believer who hasn't yet received the baptism of the Holy Spirit. My purpose here isn't to theologically break down every Scripture about this subject; I simply want to help prepare your heart for this amazing gift God has for you.

Without the baptism of the Spirit, you won't be able to experience and live in the fullness of what I've shared in this book. It's essential for fulfilling your God-given calling and to experience all that's yours in Christ. The word *baptize* in the original Greek is "baptizo," which means to dunk, submerge, saturate, and overwhelm. Do you want to be dunked, submerged, saturated, and overwhelmed by the Spirit of God? Trust me, you do.

There are many evidences of the baptism of the Spirit, and the most common is speaking in tongues. Chapter 13 details my experience with this for the first time. Speaking in tongues isn't only for ministers and missionaries, and it hasn't passed away with the first apostles—it's a vibrant, living gift for us to receive today. It's in the Word of God, and if this gift was good enough for the first church, it's good enough for us too! Let's look at Jesus' words about receiving the Holy Spirit.

"Let me ask you this: Do you know of any father who would give his son a snake on a plate when he asked for a serving of fish? Of course not! Do you

know of any father who would give his daughter a spider when she had asked for an egg? Of course not! If imperfect parents know how to lovingly take care of their children and give them what they need, how much more will the perfect heavenly Father give the Holy Spirit's fullness when His children ask Him?"

(Luke 11:11-13 TPT).

Just like every other gift from God, this one comes the same way: *by grace through faith.* You were saved by grace through faith, and you receive the Holy Spirit by grace through faith. Jesus told us to ask God, and He plainly expressed the willing heart of your heavenly Father to freely give without holding back. If you ask Him, He will freely give you the fullness of His Spirit without measure. Ask Him for this beautiful, life-changing gift, and simply receive it by faith. Receiving is as easy as breathing in. It is as easy as receiving a gift on Christmas day. Even if you don't feel any goosebumps or have a dynamic spiritual encounter, *trust that you've received.*

The Holy Spirit won't grab your mouth and force you to speak in tongues. *The disciples spoke* as the Spirit gave them utterance (Acts 2:4). Maybe you'll hear a syllable in your head—speak it out by faith. Or maybe you'll feel a stirring in your spirit that needs to be released— release it! You may feel stupid at first, that's normal—we all do. Move past the barrier of the mind and speak in tongues by faith. In time, a spiritual language will develop between you and God. It is an intimate language. It is a strategic language. God gave us this gift for a reason, and you'd be wise to use it.

Most authors would include a "repeat after me" prayer to receive the baptism of the Spirit here. But I did not feel the need to do that, because it's as easy as asking God and opening your heart to receive. Tell Him how you feel. Once you've received this glorious gift, don't neglect it. How often do we receive gifts from people and put them in our closets or under the bed, never truly enjoying the gift? Honor this tool that God has freely given to you by using it frequently. Build yourself up in your most holy faith by praying in the Spirit (Jude 1:20).

Endnotes

Chapter 1: Destined for Glory

1. Heidi Baker, *Compelled by Love* (Lake Mary, FL: Charisma House, 2008), 24-25.

Chapter 2: Pleasures of God

1. James Strong, *Strong's Concordance*, Blue Letter Bible, https://www.blueletterBible.org/lang/lexicon/lexicon.cfm?Strongs=H5731&t=NASB, H5731.

2. C.S. Lewis, *Mere Christianity* (London: Harper Collins Publ., 2015), 51.

3. Mike Bickle, *Seven Longings of the Human Heart* (Kansas City, MO: Forerunner Books, 2006), 20.

Chapter 4: Is Jesus Enough?

1. Dutch Sheets, *The Pleasure of His Company: A Journey to Intimate Friendship with God* (Bloomington, MN: Bethany House Publishers, 2014), 149.

Chapter 5: Divine Hunger

1. Bickle, *Seven Longings of the Human Heart*, 11.

2. Bill Johnson, *Experience the Impossible: Simple Ways to Unleash Heaven's Power on Earth* (Ada, MI: Chosen Books, 2014), 131.

Chapter 6: Faith's Access

1. Brother Lawrence, *The Practice of the Presence*

of God (Uhrichsville, OH: Barbour Publishing, Inc, 2004), 20.

2. Smith Wigglesworth, *Greater Works: Experiencing God's Power* (New Kensington, PA: Whitaker House, 2000), 483.

3. Warren W. Wiersbe and Lloyd M. Perry, *The Wycliffe Handbook of Preaching and Preachers* (Chicago: Moody Press, 1984), 242.

4. David Wilkerson, *Hungry for More of Jesus* (Ada, MI: Chosen Books, 1992), 59.

Chapter 7: Embrace Grace

1. Strong, *Strong's Concordance,* Blue Letter Bible, http://www.Bibletools.org/index.cfm/fuseaction /Lexicon.show/ID/G5485/charis.htm, 5485.

Chapter 8: Condemnation Free

1. Bill Johnson, *Dreaming with God: Secrets to Redesigning Your World with God's Creative Flow* (Shippensburg, PA: Destiny Image Publishers, 2006), 55.

2. *Merriam-Webster Dictionary*, s.v. "Shame," http://www.merriam-webster.com/dictionary/ shame.

Chapter 13: Practicing the Spirit

1. Brian Simmons, *Psalms: Poetry on Fire, The Passion Translation* (Savage, MN: BroadStreet Publishing Group, 2014), endnote *a*, loc. 37.

2. Brother Lawrence, *The Practice of the Presence of* God, 34.

About Michael Lombardo

Michael Lombardo is an international minister, revivalist, and author. After a radical encounter with Jesus, his life was powerfully transformed from being a drug junkie to becoming a lover of God. He attended and graduated from Christ for the Nations Institute in Dallas, Texas, and it was there that he was ignited with a passion for overseas missions. Since then, he has preached the gospel with salvations, signs, and wonders in over twelve nations. He met his wife, Selina, while serving with Iris Global in the bush of Mozambique. Michael and Selina are now the founders of Life Poured Out International, a mission-centered ministry with a vision to reach the lost, ignite the church, and care for the poor and orphan. Their ministry is marked with a tangible move of God's Spirit, prophecy, healing, and manifestations of God's glory. Their aim is to reveal the love of God, grace of Christ, and powerful presence of the Holy Spirit wherever they go. In December 2015, their lives were graced with the birth of their first child, a baby girl, Selah Gloria. They are lovers of God with an unrelenting passion to spread Christ's love across the nations. Currently, they are based in New Jersey.

Visit us Online:

www.Lifepouredoutintl.org

Find Michael on Social Media:

Personal FB page: /mikelombardo1

Ministry FB page: @lifepouredoutintl

instagram.com/lifepouredoutintl

twitter.com/_lifepouredout_

Give Online:

www.Lifepouredoutintl.org/giving

Book Michael to minister at your church, conference or upcoming event:

Email us at lifepouredoutintl@gmail.com

FREE E-BOOKS?
YES, PLEASE!

Get **FREE** and deeply-discounted **Christian books** for your **e-reader** delivered to your inbox **every week!**

IT'S SIMPLE!

VISIT lovetoreadclub.com

SUBSCRIBE by entering your email address

RECEIVE free and discounted e-book offers and inspiring articles delivered to your inbox every week!

Unsubscribe at any time.

SUBSCRIBE NOW!

visit **LOVETOREADCLUB.COM** ▶